weekend projects

SOFT FURNISHINGS

weekend projects

SOFT FURNISHINGS

CHRIS JEFFERYS

NH
NEW
HOLLAND

Published in 2013 by
New Holland Publishers
London • Sydney • Cape Town • Auckland

Garfield House 86–88 Edgware Road London W2 2EA United Kingdom
1/66 Gibbes Street Chatswood NSW 2067 Australia
Wembley Square First Floor Solan Road Gardens Cape Town 8001 South Africa
218 Lake Road Northcote Auckland New Zealand

www.newhollandpublishers.com

ISBN: 978 1 78009 514 1

Publisher: Fiona Schultz
Design: Lorena Susak
Photographer: Shona Wood
Illustrations: Coral Mula
Production Director: Olga Dementiev
Printer: Toppan Leefung Printing Ltd (China)

10 9 8 7 6 5 4 3 2 1

Follow New Holland Publishers on
Facebook: www.facebook.com/NewHollandPublishers

Contents

Introduction 6
Materials and equipment 8
Basic techniques 11

Introduction

Soft furnishings are a quick and easy way to change or update the colourscheme of a room. It could be the simplest thing – a drape around the window, a throw over a sofa and some new cushions will do the trick in next to no time. There are of course some more complex soft furnishing projects where the wide choice of fabrics available will make it possible to change to a new colourscheme at a fraction of the cost of buying ready-made items. By making your own soft furnishings, you have the reward of designing and creating your own look to suit your taste and lifestyle and the chance to work with a wonderful array of fabric colours and textures. The projects in this book vary from simple cushions and bedcovers to more sophisticated bolsters and fitted covers, so there is always an option for the beginner as well as the more experienced stitcher. For those new to making their own soft furnishings, there is a basics section that includes step-by-step colour photographs to take you through all the techniques needed to complete the projects successfully, from basic pinning to inserting zippers and trimming with piping.

The projects are designed for maximum style combined with simplicity: if there is an easy way to create a look, you'll find it here. The book is divided into sections according to how the items are be used. The Chairs section contains stylish cushions, luxurious throws and gorgeous seat covers that are easy to make and elegant.

In Tables, there are tablecloths, both round and square, with a choice of lovely decorative edges, a great napkin collection and elegant table runners to add style to the smartest table settings.

The Beds section has a full selection of pillowcase and duvet designs, an amazingly simple canopy and bedhead and a straightforward but stunning patchwork quilt as well as valances and bedcovers.

The Windows chapter combines a wonderful array of window treatments with easy-to-make, almost no-sew drapes, and lined and unlined curtains that use tab tops and clip tops as well as conventional headings. I have included quick ways to line curtains and make pelmets as well as the more traditional methods. There are roller blinds and Roman blinds, including a really quick method that does away with all those battens and rings.

Whatever your level of experience, I am sure you will find plenty of inspiration and essential practical advice in the projects that follow.

Materials and equipment

Bias binding
This is a strip of fabric cut on the cross grain and comes with the edges pressed over ready for use. It is available in cotton and satin in various widths.

Blind cord
A strong, fine cord that is threaded through the blind rings and used to raise or lower the blind.

Blind rings
Small plastic or brass rings that are stitched to the wrong side of Roman and festoon blinds as part of the lowering and raising system.

Buttons
Often made from plastic or pearl, buttons fasten through buttonholes or loops to close an opening. Fabric-covered buttons can be made by covering metal or plastic moulds.

Curtain heading tape
A stiff tape available in different widths and styles that is stitched to the top of curtains and pulled up to form pleats or gathers.

Decorative trims
Tassels, ric-rac, piping, and ribbons are all decorative trims that can be inserted in seams or stitched to the surface of items.

Dressmaker's scissors
Bent-handled dressmaker's scissors or shears are the most comfortable to use for cutting fabric accurately as the angle of the handle allows the fabric to lie flat.

Dressmaking pins
Pins are available with metal, glass or pearlized heads. Pins with coloured heads are easier to spot and pick up, though selecting pins which are fine and sharp is the main importance. Extra-fine pins are available for lace.

Erasable marker
Air-erasable and water-erasable marker pens are a useful addition to your sewing kit. Air-erasable marks disappear after a fairly short time. Water-erasable marks will remain until washed away.

Eyelets
Chrome or brass metal rings are used to make holes in fabric to thread a pole or cord through or simply as a decorative feature.

Lining fabric
Used to line curtains when required to give extra weight and body. Lining can also be used to cover the wrong side of an item when it will not show.

Needles
Various types of needles are available and a mixed pack of multi-purpose needles is often the best option. Choose needles that are fine and sharp with eyes large enough to thread easily. Extra-fine needles are also available.

Press-stud tape
A tape with poppers ready attached at intervals. Used to fasten long openings such as duvet cover openings.

Ruler

A metal or plastic ruler is handy to measure and mark short distances and as a guide for drawing straight lines.

Small scissors or snips

Small sharp scissors or special snips are useful for snipping thread ends and can be used close to the fabric where larger scissors would be unwieldy.

Tape measure

A plastic-coated or cloth tape measure is used to measure longer distances and around curves. A retractable tape measure is a neat option.

Thread

Multi-purpose polyester thread for use on all types of fabric is available in a wide range of colours. Cotton and silk thread is also available for use on their respective fabrics. Invisible thread is a strong nylon thread and buttonhole twist or bold thread is a thicker, stronger thread, useful for hand-sewing heavier fabrics.

Velcro

A fastener that comes in two parts, with hooks on one and soft loops on the other, which stick together when closed. Available in strip form or spots and for sewing or sticking on.

Zippers

These are fasteners with metal or plastic teeth that interlock together when the zipper tag is pulled over them. Used widely in openings for cushion covers.

SEWING MACHINE

Most sewing machines are run by electricity through a foot pedal, which is attached by one cable to the machine and another to the electricity supply. Pressure on the foot pedal will start the machine going and, as more pressure is added, the speed will increase. A hand wheel at the right of the machine is also usually employed when starting and stopping a piece of machine-stitching to help control and smooth the process.

Machine-stitching is formed from two threads: the top thread and the bobbin thread. Thread is first wound from the thread reel onto the bobbin by a system usually situated on the machine. The top thread slots through a number of guides and down and through the needle. The wound bobbin is placed into the bobbin case, which is under the needle. During the stitching, the top thread forms the stitch on the top of the fabric and the bobbin thread forms the stitch on the underside with the two interlinking within the fabric.

Needles for sewing machines come in a variety of different sizes. The lower the number, the finer the needle point.

Basic techniques

This section takes you through all the essential techniques needed to complete the projects in this book, from pinning and tacking to more advanced techniques such as piping. Once mastered, the basics will be used again and again to complete rewarding projects.

Pinning, tacking and hand stitches

PINNING AND TACKING
Crossways pinning

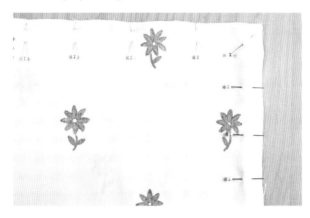

Pin together the edges to be joined at right angles to the edge. Place the pins about 5 cm (2 in) apart; on firm fabric you can space them further apart. Pin diagonally at corners.

Lengthways pinning

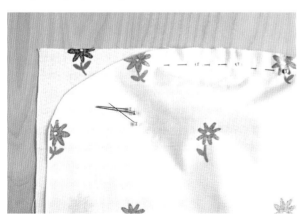

Lengthways pins are placed along the seamline where it will be stitched. This method can be more effective in tricky areas such as fitting a curved edge to a straight edge. When tacking or stitching, remove these pins as you reach them.

Pinning hems
Hems can be pinned with crossways pins or with pins lying in the same direction as the inner fold of the hem. Crossways pins are more effective if any fullness is being eased in, such as on a curved hem. Remove the pins when tacking or stitching, in the same way as before.

Tacking (Basting)
Using sewing thread or special tacking thread, begin and finish tacking with one or two backstitches. Make stitches 1–1.5 cm (⅜–⅝ in) long. Work the tacking over crossways pins and remove the pins afterwards. Or, on lengthways pinning, remove the pins as you reach them.

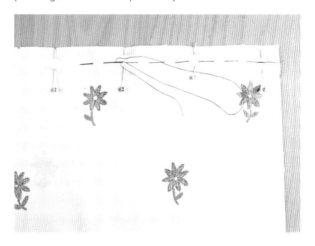

HANDSTITCHES
Backstitches

These stitches are worked one on top of the other and are used to start and finish handstitching. When tacking, the stitches can be 6 mm (¼ in) long. In other areas it is best to make them as small as possible and position them where they are least noticeable. Insert the needle into the fabric and out again, return the needle to the beginning and work two or three more stitches on top of the first one.

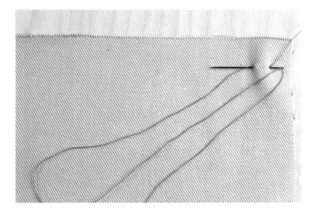

Slip hem

Used to stitch hems and the inner edge of bias binding. Begin with backstitches near the fold of the hem. Make a stitch picking up just a thread of fabric above the hem, then stitch along diagonally through the hem again, taking care not to pull too tight. When stitching binding, the stitch can pass through the back of the machine stitching.

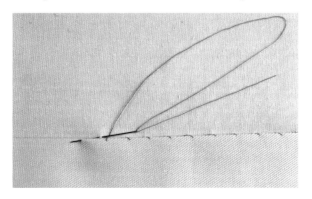

Slipstitch

This stitch is used to sew lining to curtains. Make each stitch about 1.5 cm (⅝ in) long. Slide the needle along under the main fabric then out to pick up a couple of threads at the edge of the lining. Take the needle back to the main fabric and slide it along again to make the next stitch.

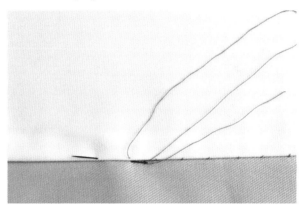

Ladder stitch

This is used to stitch two butting folded edges together. Start with backstitches, then take the needle along inside the fold of one edge for about 3–6 mm (⅛–¼ in). Bring the needle out at the fold, take it directly across to the other fold edge and stitch along inside that fold in the same way. Repeat.

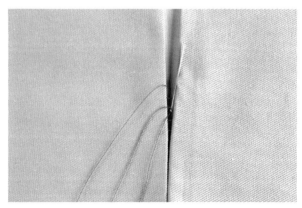

Blanket stitch

A decorative stitch, used to finish the edges of blankets and throws on fabrics that do not fray. Work from left to right. Begin with backstitches on the wrong side and bring the needle out to the right side about 12 mm–1.5 cm (½–⅝ in) in from the edge. Moving the needle along about 12 mm (½ in), take it through to the wrong side and downwards so that its point projects beyond the fabric edge. Loop the thread under the needle, then pull the needle through. Repeat. At each corner, work three stitches into the same hole as shown.

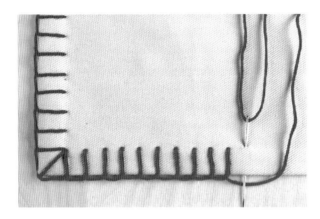

Long stitch

This is used to stitch the side hems on interlined curtains where it holds the hem to the interlining. Make a horizontal stitch across from right to left, then take the needle down diagonally for about 4 cm (1½ in) and repeat.

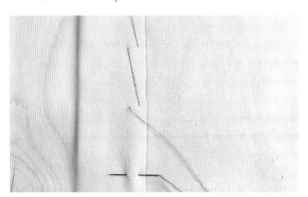

Herringbone stitch

Used to stitch hems on interlined curtains and to join butted edges of wadding (batting) and interlining. Work from left to right and begin with backstitches. Bring the needle through the hem, take it diagonally up to the right and take a stitch through above the hem from right to left. Bring the needle diagonally down to the right and take a stitch through the hem from right to left. Repeat.

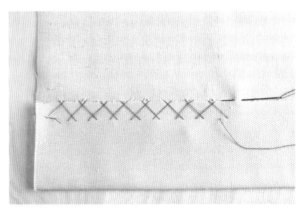

Lockstitch

Used to stitch interlining to curtain fabric. Fold back the interlining as required. Backstitch on the interlining to begin, move the needle along and take a stitch through the fold of the interlining. Leave a thread loop like blanket stitch and take a small stitch to pick up the curtain fabric within this loop. Pull the stitch through but do not pull it tight. Space the stitches at intervals of about 10 cm (4 in).

Seams and hems

Less experienced stitchers may wish to pin and tack (baste) their work before stitching, while those with more confidence may prefer to pin and remove the pins as the stitching reaches them.

Plain seam

A plain seam is used to join two pieces of fabric together. It can be pressed open when joining widths of fabric or left with the edges together, such as around the edge of a cushion. The seam allowance is usually 1.5 cm (⅝ in) wide. If it varies, this will be stated in the instructions.

1 Place the fabric pieces together with right sides facing and raw edges level. Stitch along 1.5 cm (⅝ in) in from the edge.

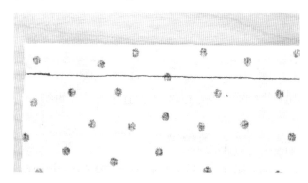

2 Open out the fabric and press the seam open, using the point of the iron. If the raw edges are exposed, zigzag stitch along each edge to neaten.

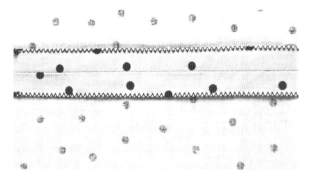

Narrow seam

This type of seam is used on sheer fabrics, as it is neater and less noticeable than a seam pressed open.

Stitch the seam as for a Plain seam, step 1. Trim both seam allowances together to about half their original width. Zigzag stitch the two raw edges together. Open out the fabric and press the seam to one side.

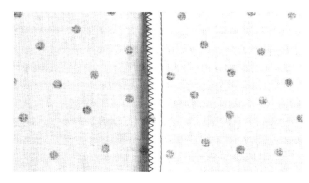

Trimming and snipping

The seam allowances are usually left intact, but if they cause too much bulk at the edge of an item, they can be trimmed to about half their original width. **Outer corners** First make a diagonal cut across the corner, then cut away wedges from each side of the diagonal cut.

Inner corners On an internal corner, snip into the corner to a few threads from the stitching, but take care not to snip too close to the stitching.

Curves On a concave curve, snip into the seam allowance so that the seam allowance can expand when turned right side out. On a convex curve, cut out small wedge-shaped notches. The tighter the curve, the closer together the notches and snips should be.

Flat fell seam

A flat fell seam is used to join fabrics where a strong, easy-to-launder seam is required.

1 Place the two edges wrong sides together and raw edges level. Stitch 1.5 cm (⅝ in) in from the edge. Trim one seam allowance to 6 mm (¼ in).

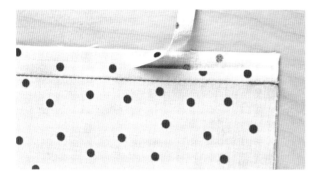

2 Open out the fabric and press the seam so the wider seam allowance lies on top of the trimmed one. Tuck the wider seam allowance under the trimmed edge and press. Stitch close to the pressed fold. The finished seam has two rows of stitching.

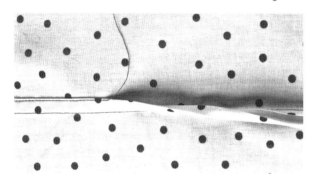

Basic hem
Press 1–1.5 cm (⅜–⅝ in) to the wrong side, then turn up the hem depth and stitch in place.

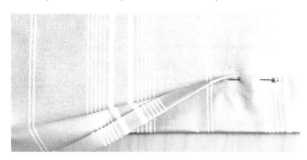

Double hem
This type of hem is used on sheer fabrics to conceal the inner layer of the hem. First press the hem depth to the wrong side, then press the same amount again and stitch in place.

Blind hemstitched hem
Most machines have a blind hemstitch, which consists of a few straight stitches followed by a wide zigzag stitch. The straight stitches are worked along the hem edge and the zigzag stitch catches the hem to the main fabric. The stitch can be fiddly to set up accurately, but is worth the effort when stitching long lengths.

Form the hem as described above. Then, with the wrong side uppermost, fold back the hem under the main fabric with the hem edge projecting and stitch in place.

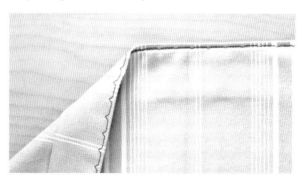

Bias binding and piping

BIAS BINDING

Bias binding can be bought or made. To make your own bias strips for both binding and covering piping cord, cut strips four times the required finished width diagonally across the fabric. For binding, press both long edges in so that they almost meet at the centre.

Joining strips

1 Open out the binding folds and trim the two ends on the straight grain. Place the two ends together with right sides facing, the straight ends level and the foldlines intersecting 6 mm (¼ in) in. Pin to hold. Stitch the two ends together, taking a 6 mm (¼ in) seam.

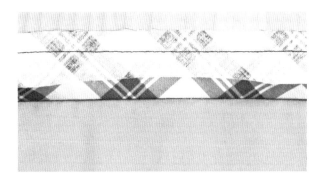

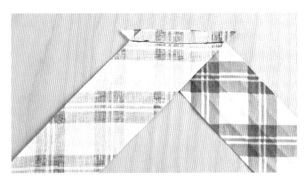

2 Open out the binding and press the seam open. Trim off the corners of the seam level with the edge of the binding and re-press the binding folds.

2 Fold the other edge of the binding over to the wrong side so that its edge is level with the machine stitching and stitch in place by hand.

Binding an edge

1 Unfold one edge of the binding and place the raw edge level with the fabric edge on the right side of the fabric. Stitch in place along the fold.

Sandwich method

Fold and press the binding in half so that the upper half, which will be on the right side, is just narrower than the lower half. Sandwich the fabric into the binding and stitch from the right side.

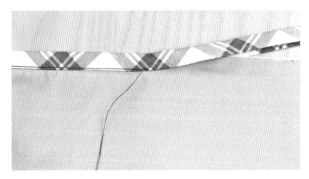

Double binding method

This is a neat method for lighter-weight fabrics and wider bindings.

1 Cut the bias strip six times the required finished width and press the binding in half lengthways. Place the raw edges level with the fabric edge on the wrong side and stitch in place the required width of the binding in from the edge.

2 Fold the other edge over to the right side so that it just covers the stitching and machine-stitch in place.

Joining ends

Join the ends with a diagonal seam before the stitching is complete, using the same method as for joining lengths of bias binding.

Alternatively, an easier method is to overlap the finishing end over the starting end, tucking the raw end under as shown, and then complete the stitching.

Using bought bias binding

Ready-made bias binding can be found in a range of colours and is also available with a satin finish as well as in plain cotton. It is also available in a variety of widths and some specialist haberdashers will have patterned bias binding (see Roller blind with scalloped border, page 144). It comes ready folded and is attached in the same way as for homemade binding strips.

PIPING

Piping can be bought ready-made with a projecting flange to insert into a seam or it can be made by covering piping cord with a strip of bias-cut fabric.

Stitching piping

1 Cut the bias strip wide enough to fit around the cord plus two seam allowances of 1.5 cm (⅝ in). Wrap the strip around the cord and, using a zipper foot, stitch along close to the cord but not right next to it.

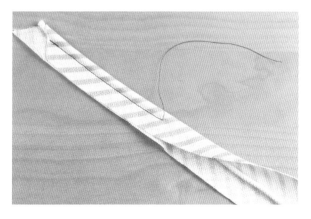

2 Place the piping onto the right side of one fabric layer and stitch in place along the line of the first stitching.

3 Sandwich the piping with the other layer of the seam. Then turn the piece over so that the previous stitching is uppermost. Stitch in place just inside the previous stitching so that the first two rows will be hidden.

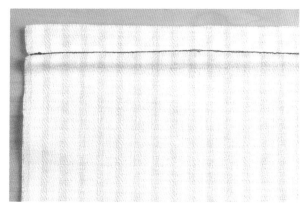

Piping around a corner

Snip the flat flange 1.5 cm (⅝ in) in from the corner so that it will open out to fit around the corner, ensuring that the raw edges are level with the next edge. If the corner is curved, make three snips around it.

Joining piping ends, method one

1 Leave about 2.5 cm (1 in) unstitched at each end of the piping. Cut the piping so that it overlaps the first end by 2 cm (¾ in). Unpick the end of the piping to reveal the cord and snip away the cord only, so that it butts up to the beginning end of the cord.

2 Fold under 1 cm (⅜ in) on the overlapping end of the piping and lap it over the beginning of the piping. Then complete the stitching, overlapping the beginning of the stitching line.

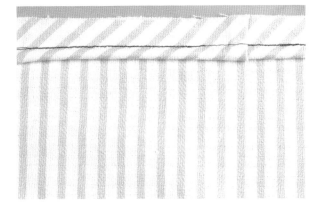

Joining piping ends, method two

With this method, the ends of the piping are overlapped at an angle and finished inside the seam. This method can also be used for purchased piping where it is not possible to cut away the inner piping cord. In this case, press the overlapped ends as flat as possible before stitching across them.

Leave the piping unstitched for 2.5 cm (1 in) on each side of the join and allow some excess at each end of the piping. Overlap the ends at the seamline, unpick the fabric covering and trim the cords where they overlap. Replace the covering and overlap the flat ends diagonally into the seam allowance. Then complete the stitching, overlapping the beginning of the stitching line.

Fringing and frills

FRINGING

Fringing can be purchased as a trim or made by pulling away the threads from a woven fabric. Some woven fabrics do not fringe well, so check before purchasing.

Applying fringing trim

1 Press a narrow turning, just wide enough to be covered by the braid part of the fringe, onto the right side.

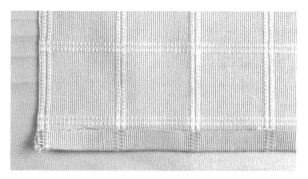

2 Arrange the fringing braid along the turning to cover it. Stitch in place with a row of stitching near the fabric edge and another just above the raw edge so that it is enclosed.

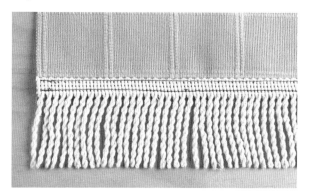

Fringing fabric

A fringe can be made by simply pulling the fabric threads away from the fabric edge. For a more durable fringe, particularly on items that will be laundered, first stitch a row of narrow zigzag stitching in a matching colour across the fabric at the top of the fringe. Then fringe the fabric back to the stitching.

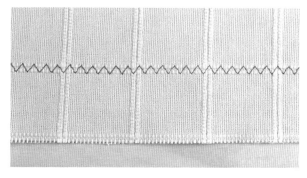

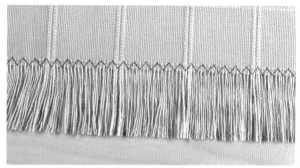

Knotting and plaiting

Both knotting and plaiting will reduce the length of a fringe considerably, so, whenever possible, test on a piece of spare fabric.

To knot, simply gather a bunch of threads together and knot them near the top of the fringe.

For a plait, gather a bunch in the same way, divide it into three sections and plait together. Finish near the base with a thread wrapped round and round and knotted firmly.

FRILLS

Frills can be made from a single layer of fabric with a hemmed edge or from fabric folded double so that no hem is needed. Those shown here are gathered, but they could be pleated. Allow 1½ times the length of the edge to be trimmed. A lace frill can be attached in the same way.

Single frill

1 Cut the frill to the required width plus 12 mm (½ in) for the hem and 1.5 cm (⅝ in) seam allowance. Press 6 mm (¼ in), then another 6 mm (¼ in) to the wrong side along one long edge of the frill and stitch in place. If the ends will show, hem them in the same way.

2 Adjust the machine stitch to its longest length and stitch along 1.5 cm (⅝ in) from the other edge. Stitch a second row of gathering 6 mm (¼ in) inside the first row. On long frills, stop and restart the stitching to divide the gathered edge up into about 75 cm (30 in) lengths.

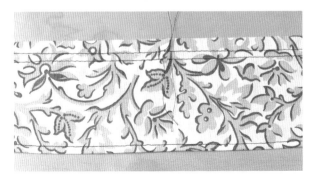

3 Divide the frill and the edge to which it will be stitched into an equal number of sections and mark with pins. With right sides facing, pin the edges together at the marker pins. Pull the gathering threads on the wrong side of the frill together while sliding the fabric along to form gathers.

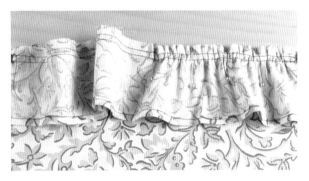

4 When gathered to fit, wind the thread ends around a pin in a figure-of-eight to hold. Adjust the gathers evenly and stitch in place just below the inner row of gathers.

Double frill

Cut the frill twice the required finished width plus 3 cm (1¼ in). If the ends will show, fold the frill in half with right sides together, stitch across the ends, then turn the frill right sides out. Press the frill in half lengthways with the right sides outside. Gather and attach the frill as for the single frill, steps 2, 3 and 4.

Borders and mitred borders

Block border

Measure the first two edges and cut borders to this length x the desired finished width plus 3 cm (1¼ in). With right sides facing, stitch the borders to the centre panel, taking 1.5 cm (⅝ in) seam allowances. Press the seams toward the borders. Measure the two remaining edges, including the ends of the first borders, and cut borders to this length and the same width. Stitch in place. Press.

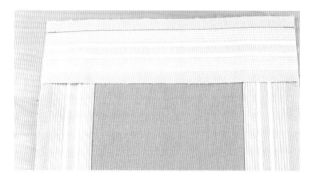

Single mitred border

Decide on the finished border width and add on 3 cm (1¼ in). For the length, measure the length of the centre panel including seam allowances and add twice the width of the finished border.

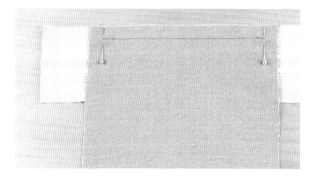

1 Match the centre of the borders to the centre edges to which they are being stitched. Stitch in place, starting and finishing 1.5 cm (⅝ in) in from the edge of the centre panel. Repeat.

2 Fold the centre panel diagonally, so that two adjoining borders are level. Draw a diagonal line from the end of the previous stitching to the outer corner of the border. Stitch along the line. Trim away the corners 1 cm (⅜ in) outside the line and press the seam open. Stitch all corners in this way. Then press the panel seams toward the borders.

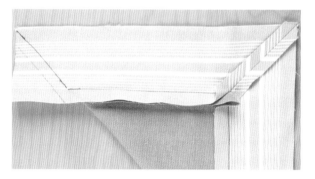

Double mitred border

Decide on the desired finished border width, double this and add on 3 cm (1¼ in) for seams. Measure the length of the centre panel including seams, plus twice the width of the finished border.
1 Fold the borders in half right sides together. Overlap the ends of two borders at right angles, with the folds on the outer edges and the ends projecting by 1.5 cm (⅝ in), and pin. Draw a diagonal line across the corner. Mark 1 cm (⅜ in) outside the line. Turn the border over and repeat on the other side. Trim along the outer lines.

2 Unpin the borders; open them out and mark the seamline on the unmarked half of each border. Place the appropriate two borders together with right sides facing and stitch along the marked lines, starting and finishing 1.5 cm (⅝ in) in from the side edges of the border. Trim the point and press the seam open. Stitch all four corners in this way.

3 Place the right side of one border edge to the wrong side of the centre panel. Pin together, making sure all four corners match, so that the end of the border stitching is 1.5 cm (⅝ in) from each edge at the corners. Stitch each edge separately, stopping and restarting at each corner.

4 Press the seam allowance to the wrong side along the remaining edge of the border. Then place it over to the right side of the centre panel so that it just covers the previous stitching and the seam is enclosed. Stitch in place.

Mitred hem

1 Press the appropriate double hem in place, then unfold. Fold the corner over diagonally level with the inner pressed corner. Press the fold and trim the corner away 1 cm (⅜ in) inside the fold.

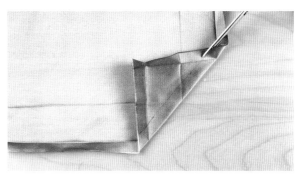

2 Refold the corners with right sides facing so that the pressed lines match. Stitch along the pressed line from the corner to finish at the outer hem fold. Press the mitre seam open. Refold the hem and press again.

Buttons, buttonholes, ties and zippers

BUTTONS

There are two main types of button: flat buttons, which have two or four holes pierced through them, and shank buttons, which have a protruding shank at the back through which they are stitched on. A shank spaces the button away from the fabric to allow fabric layers to lie flat under the button when it is fastened.

Stitching on a flat button

Using a double thread, stitch a couple of back-stitches one on top of the other at the button position. Pass the needle up through one hole, then back down through the other hole and through the fabric. Work four to six stitches in this way to secure the button. On buttons with four holes, work two parallel sets of stitches or form the stitches into a cross, then fasten off the thread with more backstitches behind the fabric.

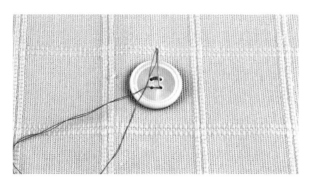

Making a shank for a flat button

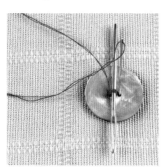

1 Stitch on the button in the same way as for a button with holes, but work over a cocktail stick or thick needle placed on top of the button as a spacer.

2 Before finishing off, take the thread through to between the button and the fabric. Remove the spacer and wind the thread around the stitches between the button and fabric to form a thread shank, then finish off on the reverse.

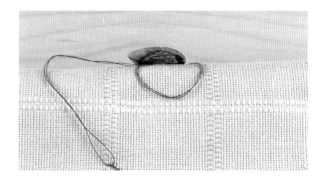

Stitching on a shank button

Using a double thread, secure the thread ends with backstitch at the button position. Stitch alternately through the shank and the fabric four to six times, then finish off with backstitches on the wrong side behind the button.

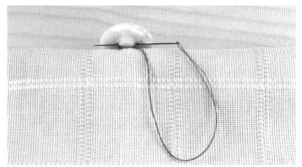

MAKING BUTTONHOLES

Buttonholes are quick and easy to work by machine. The exact method varies according to the machine model and will be explained in your manual.

Buttonholes are stitched with a close zigzag stitch, with wide stitches called bar tacks at each end and stitches half as wide along each side of the buttonhole. Cut the buttonhole along the centre after stitching, using small scissors to cut from each end towards the centre.

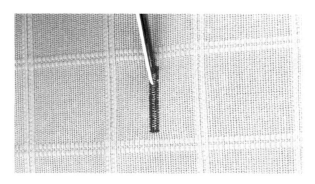

TIES

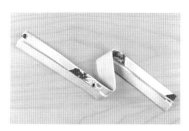

1 Press 1 cm (⅜ in) to the wrong side across one short end, or both ends if they are exposed, and along both long edges.

2 Fold the tie in half lengthways and press again. Stitch down the length of the tie. On wide ties, stitch across the pressed end as well. On narrow 12 mm (½ in) wide ties, the end can be left unstitched.

ZIPPERS

1 Stitch the seam at each end of the zipper position, leaving an opening the length of the zipper teeth. Press the seam open and the turnings to the wrong side across the opening edges. Working with right sides uppermost, pin and tack (baste) the zipper behind the opening so that one edge of the opening is just outside the zipper teeth. Using a zipper foot, stitch in place near the edge.

2 Arrange the other edge of the opening level with the stitching. Pin then tack this edge to the zipper tape. Stitch in place across each end and along the zipper tape as shown.

Pleats and tucks

PLEATS

Pleated edgings make attractive trims and are a little more tailored than gathered edgings. Pleats can be left unpressed so that they are held only at the top edge, or they can be pressed in place down their length for a more formal look.

Making knife pleats

Measure and mark the depth of the pleats at the top edge with pins or an erasable marker. Fold one marking over to meet the other. Pin, then tack (baste) along the seamline at the top edge. Stitch across the top edge to hold the pleats in place.

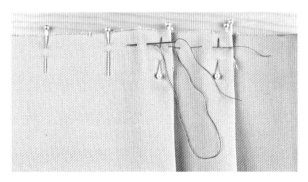

Box pleats

Box pleats are formed from two pleats facing away from each other. Measure and mark the depth of the pleats at the top edge with pins or an erasable marker. Fold the two inner markings outwards away from each other to meet the outer markings. Pin then tack along the seamline at the top edge.

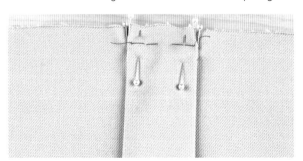

Inverted pleats

These are formed from two pleats facing toward each other so that the two folds meet at the centre of the pleat. Measure and mark the depth of the pleats at the top edge with pins or an erasable marker pen. Fold the two outer markings inward toward each other to meet at the centre marking. Pin then tack along the seam line at the top edge.

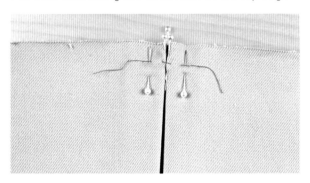

Pressed pleats

Measure and mark the pleats at intervals down the entire length of the pleat. Form the pleats and press, removing the pins as you reach them. Tack or stitch across the top edge to hold the pleats in place.

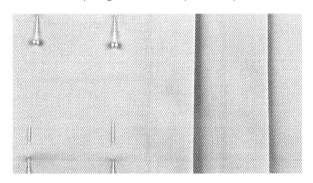

TUCKS

Tucks are stitched folds of fabric formed for a decorative effect and work particularly well with semi-sheer fabrics, as the tucks will show up well against the light. The distance of the stitching from the fold determines the type of tuck. Very fine tucks are called pin tucks. When using tucks, add twice the depth of each tuck to the fabric length.

Making pin tucks

Fold the fabric along the line of the tuck with wrong sides facing and press along the fold. With the fabric still folded, stitch along 3 mm (⅛ in) in from the fold using the machine foot as a guide. Open out the fabric and press the tuck to one side. A series of parallel pin tucks are more effective than single ones.

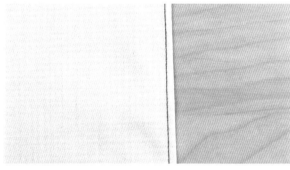

Wide tucks

Fold the fabric along the line of the tuck and press along the fold. Measure the depth of the tuck away from the fold with pins or an erasable marker pen. Tack (baste), then stitch along the tacked line. Alternatively, stitch keeping the fabric fold against one of the guidelines on the plate beside the machine foot to keep the stitching an even distance in from the fold. Open out the fabric and press the tuck to one side.

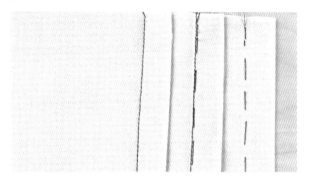

Twin needle tucks

A machine twin needle, which stitches two parallel rows, gives a fine tucked effect on lightweight fabric such as lawn. First press a crease to form a line for the tuck. Open out the fabric and stitch along the pressed crease so that it is central between the two needles.

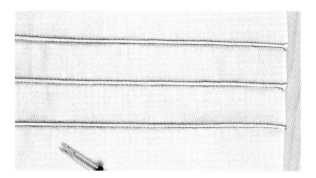

Chairs

Flap back cushion cover

This quick-and-easy method is ideal for square or rectangular cushions. The opening on the back of the cushion cover is formed by two overlapping edges between which the cushion pad is slipped in. Overlap the edges by 10 cm (4 in) on cushions up to 35 cm (13¾ in) square or by 15 cm (6 in) on larger cushions. For a rectangular cushion, place the overlap across the width of the cover rather than the length so that the opening does not gape.

MATERIALS
Silk furnishing fabric
Sewing thread
Cushion pad

CUTTING OUT
1.5 cm (⅝ in) seam allowances are included unless instructions state otherwise.

Cut out the front to the width and length of the cushion pad plus 3 cm (1¼ in). Cut out the back to the same length and 14 cm (5½ in) wider than the front, or 19 cm (7½ in) wider for a larger cushion (diagram 1).

DIAGRAM 1

Cut the back piece in half widthways (diagram 2).

DIAGRAM 2

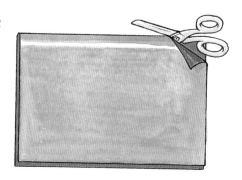

1 Press a double 1 cm (⅜ in) hem to the wrong side along the centre edges of the two back pieces. Stitch in place (diagram 3).

DIAGRAM 3

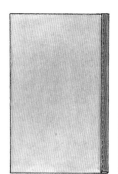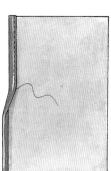

2 Place the two back pieces onto the front piece with right sides facing, arranging so that the raw edges are level all around and the hemmed edges of the back overlap. Pin together around the edge (diagram 4).

3 Stitch around the outer edge 1.5 cm (⅝ in) in from the raw edges. Trim the corners (diagram 5). Turn the cover right side out through the overlapping edges and press. Insert the cushion pad.

DIAGRAM 4

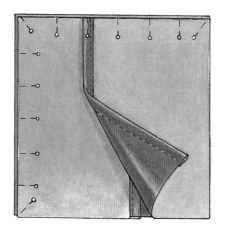

DIAGRAM 5

Variation

TWO-COLOUR CUSHION
For this easy decorative option, cut the cushion front from two fabrics in different colours, adding 1.5 cm (⅝ in) on the edges to be joined. Join the edges with a 1.5 cm (⅝ in) plain seam and press the seam open. Using machine straight stitch or zigzag stitch, stitch on ribbons parallel to the join. Stitch a few beads by hand along the edge of one ribbon to complete the effect. Make up in the same way as the Flap back cushion cover, page 30.

Cushion cover with zipper fastening

A cushion cover fastened with a zipper is a little more complicated than a flap back cover, but it has the advantage of keeping the edges of the opening pulled firmly together. You could make a feature of the zipper by placing it on the front of the cover and trimming it with beads or a tassel, or use it in a purely functional way on the back of the cover. Choose a zipper about 10 cm (4 in) shorter than the width of the cushion.

Cushion with ties

The pretty cushion is simple to make. It has a flap facing to tuck the pad behind and straight ties to hold the edges together. The facing and ties can be made from a contrast fabric or from the same fabric as the cover.

MATERIALS
Mediumweight furnishing fabric for cushion cover
Contrast fabric for facing and ties
Sewing thread
Cushion pad

CUTTING OUT
1.5 cm (⅝ in) seam allowances have been included unless instructions state otherwise.

Cut two pieces for the cover front and back the size of the cushion pad plus 3 cm (1¼ in). Cut two facing pieces the width of the cover x 12 cm (4¾ in) deep. Cut four ties 18 x 8 cm (7 x 3¼ in)

1 Make the ties by folding each tie in half lengthways with right sides together and stitching across one short edge and the long edge. Trim the seams and corners, turn the ties right side out and press.

2 Place two ties to one edge of each of the front and back pieces with the ties spaced equally and the raw edges level. Place a facing piece on top of each of the front and back pieces with right sides together and stitch together along the edge so that the ends of the ties are enclosed in the seams (diagram 1).

DIAGRAM 1

3 Open out the facings away from the cushion and press the seams open. Place the front and back right sides together and the facing seams matching exactly. Stitch the front and back together around three sides including the sides of the facing (diagram 2).

DIAGRAM 2

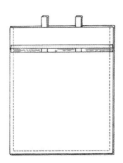

4 Trim the corners and turn the cushion cover right side out. Stitch a narrow double hem to the wrong side around the edge of the facing. Press the facing inside the cushion so that the seam is at the edge. Open the side seams out and, working from the right side, stitch down each side seam through both the cover and facing to hold the facing in place (diagram 3). Insert the cushion pad.

DIAGRAM 3

Gathered-end bolster

This long, cylindrical cushion can be made with a simple plain seam at each end, but its shape is defined more crisply if a fine piping is inserted around the seam. The circular ends are gathered and finished with a button in this version. A bolster with flat ends is given on pages 40–41. There is a zipper opening in the seam at the back of the cushion.

MATERIALS
Furnishing fabric
Sewing thread
Zipper about 7 cm (2¾ in) shorter than bolster pad
Piping cord
2 fabric-covered buttons
Bolster pad

CUTTING OUT
1.5 cm (⅝ in) seam allowances are included unless instructions state otherwise.

Measure around the circumference of the bolster pad and along the pad's length. Add on 3 cm (1¼ in) to each measurement and cut the main pieces to this size. Cut the two rectangular end pieces to the same circumference x half the diameter of the ends plus 3 cm (1¼ in).

1 Cover the piping cord with bias strips of fabric, see Piping, page 18. Place the two lengthways edges of the main piece together with right sides facing and stitch for about 5 cm (2 in) at each end, leaving an opening at the centre the length of the zipper teeth. Stitch the zipper in place, taking care to keep the underlayer out of the way, see Zippers, page 25. Stitch the piping around each end of the main piece.

2 Stitch the short edges of the end pieces together and press the seams open. With right sides facing and seams matching, stitch the end pieces around the ends of the main piece (diagram 1).

DIAGRAM 1

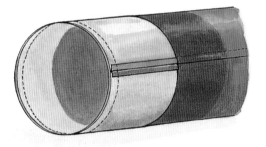

3 Open out the end pieces. Press 1.5 cm (⅝ in) to the wrong side around the remaining edge of each end piece. Using a double thread, work running stitch around the edge and pull up the thread to gather the ends in tightly (diagram 2). Finish the thread securely and stitch on a covered button at the centre. Insert the bolster pad.

DIAGRAM 2

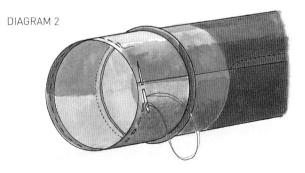

Seat pad with skirt

This style of seat pad has a flat skirt of fabric that protrudes over the chair seat around the front and side edges. It is fastened to the chair uprights with ties at the back. The seat area is padded with mediumweight wadding, but you could substitute 12 mm (½ in) foam for extra padding if you wish. If you are using a patterned fabric, arrange the pattern to run from the front to the back of the seat.

MATERIALS

Furnishing fabric
Sewing thread
Mediumweight wadding (batting)

CUTTING OUT

1.5 cm (⅝ in) seam allowances are included unless instructions state otherwise.

Measure the seat size, then add on 13 cm (5⅛ in) to the width and 8 cm (3¼ in) to the depth from front to back. Cut out two pieces of fabric to these measurements. You may need to cut out a section at the back corners to accommodate the chair uprights. Cut four fabric ties 36 cm (14 in) by 5 cm (2 in).

1 Make four ties, see Ties, page 25. Place the ties onto the right side of the pad front, positioning them in pairs at each back corner so that they match the chair uprights. Arrange the ends of the ties level with the raw edge and stitch in place 1.5 cm (⅝ in) from the edge (diagram 1).

DIAGRAM 1

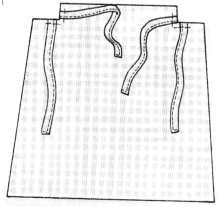

2 Place the back and front pad pieces together with right sides facing. Stitch the pieces together 1.5 cm (⅝ in) from the edges, beginning and finishing on the back edge 5 cm (2 in) in from the corners (diagram 2). Trim the corners, turn the pad right side out and press the seam at the edge.

DIAGRAM 2

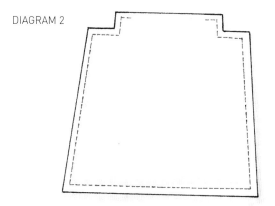

3 Beginning and finishing at the back edge, stitch around the sides and front edge of the pad, 5 cm (2 in) in from the edge, to form the skirt (diagram 3).

DIAGRAM 3

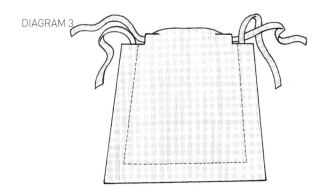

Box cushion

This piped cushion cover with a gusset can be used to re-cover an existing seat pad or fitted over a new foam pad. It has a zipper opening at the back of the gusset, so that it can easily be removed for cleaning. Choose a zipper length about one third of the whole gusset length.

MATERIALS

Furnishing fabric
Sewing thread
Zipper, about one third of gusset length
Piping cord
Foam pad

CUTTING OUT

1.5 cm (⅝ in) seam allowances are included unless instructions state otherwise.

Cut out a top and base piece to the size of the foam plus 1.5 cm (⅝ in) all around. Measure around the foam for the required finished gusset length. Cut the zipped section of the gusset the length of the zipper plus 5 cm (2 in) x the foam depth plus 6 cm (2¼ in). Then cut this section in half along its length. Cut the other section of the gusset the remainder of the length plus 3 cm (1¼ in) x the foam depth plus 3 cm (1¼ in).

NOTE

You can buy foam from specialist foam suppliers, who will cut it to size for you. Ask for advice on the most suitable type of foam and, if possible, choose a medium-density, flame-resistant type.

1 With right sides facing and raw edges level, stitch two long edges of the zipper gussets together for 2.5 cm (1 in) at each end, leaving an opening the length of the zipper teeth at the centre. Stitch the zipper into the opening, see Zippers, page 25 (diagram 1).

DIAGRAM 1

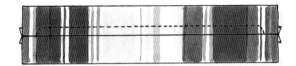

2 With right sides facing and raw edges level, stitch the short edges of the long gusset to the short edges of the zipper gusset. Press the seams open (diagram 2).

DIAGRAM 2

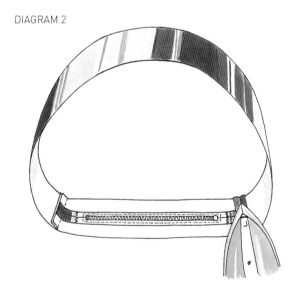

3 Stitch the piping around the edges of the top and the base pieces, see Piping, page 18.

4 Divide the edges of the top and base pieces into quarters and mark with pins (diagram 3). In the same way, mark both edges of the gusset into quarters.

DIAGRAM 3

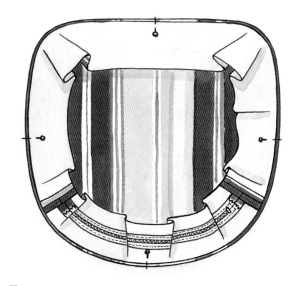

5 Open the zipper. Place the top edge of the gusset to the top piece with right sides facing and raw edges level. Match the marker pins and pin together at these points, then pin between the markers.

6 For a cover with rounded corners, make several snips close together into the gusset seam allowance at each curve – the tighter the curve, the closer the snips need to be (diagram 4).

DIAGRAM 4

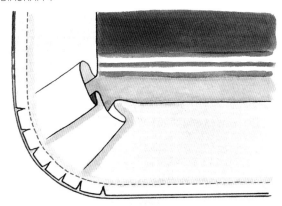

7 On a cushion cover with square corners, make a single snip into the gusset seam allowance at each corner, so that the allowance will open out to fit around the corner (diagram 5). Tack (baste), then stitch the gusset in place. Stitch the base to the other edge of the gusset in the same way. Turn right side out and press. Insert the foam pad.

DIAGRAM 5

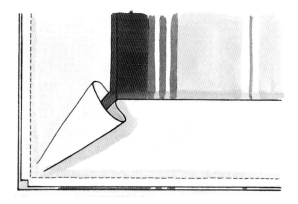

Variation

A box cushion can be made in almost any shape – just make sure that you make an accurate template of the seat area before you start.

Throw with mitred border

The double mitred border on this throw looks as good on the back as on the front. This is a very useful method of trimming reversible fabric, giving it a fine, professional-looking finish.

MATERIALS
Heavyweight main fabric, such as velvet, wool or chenille
Border fabric
Sewing thread

CUTTING OUT
1.5 cm (⅝ in) seam allowances are included unless instructions state otherwise.

Cut the main fabric to the required size. Cut the borders 17 cm (6½ in) wide for a finished width of 7 cm (2¾ in) x the length of the centre panel plus twice the finished width of the border.

1 Stitch the borders following Double mitred border, page 22, which also explains how to work out different sizes and border widths.

Throw edging variations

THROW WITH BEADED TRIM
A whole range of ready-made trims is available – sew a double hem and then stitch on the beaded trim.

THROW WITH BLANKET STITCH
Blanket stitch is a simple hand-stitched edging for a throw, see Blanket stitch, page 13. On non-fray fabrics it can be worked directly over the edge, but even here a better finish is often achieved if a single hem to the depth of the stitching is folded to the wrong side first. This gives a firm edge and also gives a good line for keeping the stitching even. On fabrics that fray such as velvet, fold a double hem before blanket stitching over it. Use a thick thread, such as wool, or a fine ribbon, as shown here.

THROW WITH FRINGED EDGE

Before you buy the fabric, check that it will fray neatly when the threads are pulled away. On closely woven fabric the threads can just be pulled away to make a fringed edge. On loosely woven fabrics and for a more durable finish, stitch a line of narrow zigzag stitch in matching thread at the top of the fringe before fraying, see Fringing fabric, page 20.

THROW WITH BINDING

Binding gives a luxurious finish to a throw, especially if a fine satin or silk is used. If you cannot find silk or satin binding, make your own from ribbon or fabric. The double binding method will give a very smart finish if a wide binding is preferred, see Double binding method, page 17.

Tailored slip cover

This smart linen slipcover will give a new lease of life to a jaded dining room chair. It is made from natural linen with fine cream piping outlining the seat and the sides of the back. There are inverted pleats at the front corners of the skirt.

MATERIALS

Mediumweight furnishing fabric
Sewing thread
Piping cord
Contrast fabric for piping

CUTTING OUT

1.5 cm (⅝ in) seam allowances are included unless instructions state otherwise.

Decide on the desired depth of the skirt. Beginning at the top of the chair seat, measure up the back of the chair back, across the top, down the front of the chair back and across the seat to the front edge, then add on the skirt depth plus 3 cm (1¼ in). Measure across the back or seat, whichever is wider, add on 5 cm (2 in) and cut the main panel to this size. Measure the skirt around the two sides and front of the chair and add on 40 cm (16 in) for pleats and 5 cm (2 in) for side hem allowances. Cut the skirt to this length by the skirt depth plus 3 cm (1¼ in).

DIAGRAM 1

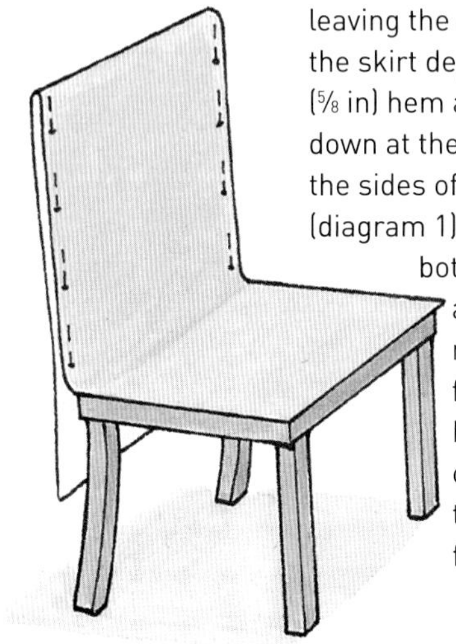

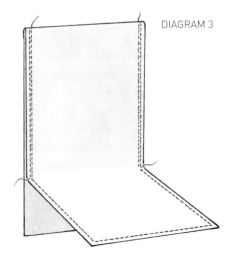

1 Try the main piece on the chair, leaving the extra fabric allowed for the skirt depth, plus 1.5 cm (⅝ in) hem allowance, hanging down at the back. Pin down the sides of the chair back (diagram 1). Check the fit on both the back and seat and adjust if required, remembering to allow for seam allowances. Mark the top edge of the chair back, then unpin the fabric and remove from the chair.

2 Cover the piping cord with bias-cut strips, see Piping, page 18, to make sufficient to fit around the sides and front of the chair seat and up the side seams on the chair back. Starting at the top of the chair back, stitch piping to the front of the main piece down one side edge, around the chair seat and back up the other side edge, finishing the ends into the seam allowance (diagram 2).

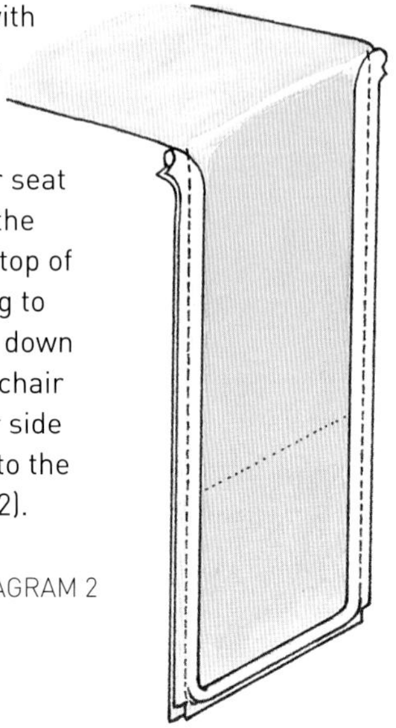

DIAGRAM 2

3 With right sides together, stitch the front to the back down the side seams, leaving the skirt depth plus 1.5 cm (⅝ in) to hang free at the base of the back (diagram 3) .

DIAGRAM 3

Tables

Square tablecloth

A classic square or rectangular tablecloth can protect a table top for everyday use or dress a table elegantly for a special meal. The square cloth shown here is finished with a deep hem for a classic look. The hem can be made on the wrong side of the fabric in the usual way for a plain look. If the fabric is reversible, you could make a feature of the hem by turning it onto the right side to give the effect of a mitred border. The finished hem is 4 cm (1½ in) deep, but you can make it narrower if you prefer.

MATERIALS

Cotton furnishing fabric
Sewing thread

CUTTING OUT

Cut out the cloth to the required size, adding 10 cm (4 in) to both the length and the width for the hem.

NOTE

Whenever possible, choose a fabric that is wide enough to make the tablecloth without joins. If joins are unavoidable, use a whole width of fabric for the centre of the cloth and add half widths, or whatever is required, to each side. Join the pieces with a flat fell seam, see Seams, page 14.

1 Press 1 cm (⅜ in), then 4 cm (1½ in) to the chosen side of the fabric to form the hem. Form and stitch mitres at the corners, see Mitred hem, page 23 (diagram 1).

DIAGRAM 1

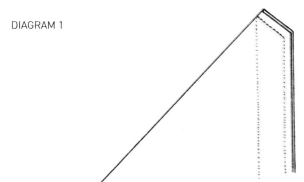

2 Refold the hem and press the corners. Pin, or tack (baste) in place if preferred, then stitch the hem along the inner fold (diagram 2).

DIAGRAM 2

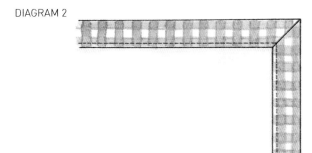

Tablecloth edging variations

TABLECLOTH WITH ORGANDIE BORDER

You will need fabric, sewing thread and organdie for the border. Cut the cloth to the required size. Cut the organdie borders 11 cm (4¼ in) wide, for a finished border width of 4 cm (1½ in) x the length of the cloth plus twice the finished border width. Make and stitch the borders as in Double mitred border, page 22, trimming all the seam allowances to 5 mm (¼ in) as they are stitched.

TABLECLOTH WITH LACE EDGING

A lace edging will add a lovely touch to a plain white tablecloth. You can buy lace trims such as broderie Anglaise in haberdashers but it is worth looking out for old lace tablecloths in antique markets that you can recycle.

Stitch a double 1 cm (⅜ in) hem around the tablecloth. Overlap the finished hem edge over the inner edge of the lace and stitch in place.

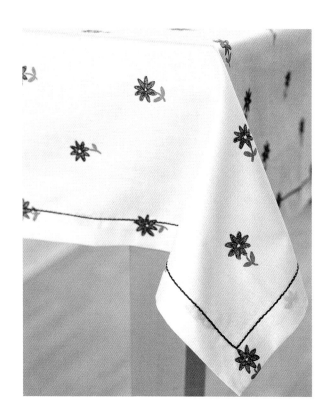

TABLECLOTH WITH ZIGZAG BORDER

You will need materials as for the basic square tablecloth plus contrasting cotton perlé or stranded cotton embroidery thread, an embroidery needle and matching sewing thread. Make the cloth as for the basic square tablecloth with the hem on the wrong side. Thread a long length of embroidery thread into the needle, bring it through to the front of the cloth from the wrong side and place it along the hem, using the stitching as a guide. Using a close machine zigzag stitch, work over the embroidery thread to create a decorative border. Finish the ends of all the threads on the wrong side.

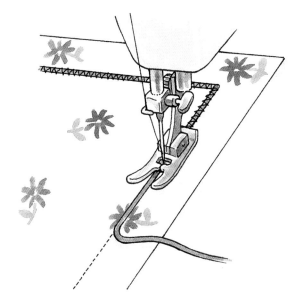

Circular tablecloth

Circular cloths are used to dress round dining tables and can be practical or luxurious depending on the fabric you choose. You can also make a feature of a small occasional table by making a circular cloth with a stylishly deep drop.

MATERIALS

Lightweight furnishing fabric
Sewing thread
Brown paper
String
Pencil

CUTTING OUT

1.5 cm (⅝ in) seam allowances are included unless instructions state otherwise.

Tie the pencil onto the end of the string. Measure and mark half the required diameter plus 1.5 cm (⅝ in) along the string from the pencil. Hold the marked string at one corner of the paper and, keeping the string taut, draw a quarter circle with the pencil (diagram 1).

Cut the paper along the drawn line. Fold the fabric into four, then place the straight edges of the pattern level with the folded edges of the fabric. Pin the paper in place and cut around the circular edge through all four layers of fabric.

DIAGRAM 1

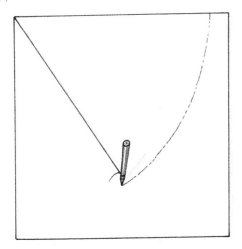

NOTE

Because of the restriction of the fabric width, most circular tablecloths need to be joined. Use a full fabric width for a central panel and stitch more fabric to each side to make up the required width. Join the pieces before cutting out, using flat fell seams if the cloth is to be laundered frequently or plain seams if the cloth is mainly decorative, see Seams, page 14.

1 Open the fabric out. Stitch around the circle 1.5 cm (⅝ in) in from the edge. Fold the raw edge over to the wrong side along the stitched line, pressing as you go. The stitching will naturally roll over to just inside the fold, giving a smooth curve.

2 Carefully turn under the raw edge to make a double hem. Press it as you go, easing in any fullness. Pin, tack (baste), then stitch the hem in place (diagram 2).

DIAGRAM 2

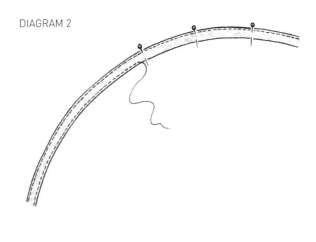

Beaded napkins

These pretty silk napkins with beaded trims are perfect for special occasions. The measurements given will make napkins with a generous finished size of 45 cm (17¾ in) square. If you prefer smaller napkins, cut the fabric 48 cm (19 in) square for a finished size of 40 cm (15¾ in)

MATERIALS
Silk fabric
Sewing thread
Small seed beads (optional)
Fine needle

CUTTING OUT
Cut out the fabric to 53 cm (21 in) square for each napkin.

1 Press 1 cm (⅜ in), then 3 cm (1¼ in) to the wrong side of the fabric to form the hem. Form and stitch mitres at the corners, see Mitred hem, page 23 (diagram 1).

DIAGRAM 1

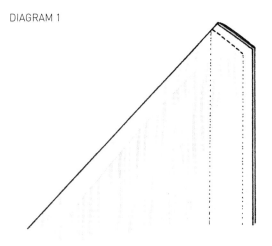

2 Stitch the hem in place. Using a fine needle, apply a row of small beads near the outer fold of the hem, spacing them about 3 cm (1¼ in) apart. Stitch each bead with two small backstitches before slipping the needle along inside the hem to the next bead position (diagram 2). Alternatively, stitch the beads in clusters of three along the centre of the hem or in radiating lines at the corners.

DIAGRAM 2

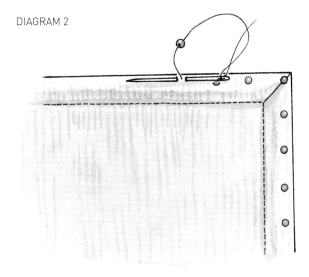

Napkin variations

CLASSIC LINEN NAPKIN

Cut out and make the napkin as in step 1 of the Beaded napkins, page 66, but fold the hem onto the right side of the fabric. Stitch the hem in place near its inner edge.

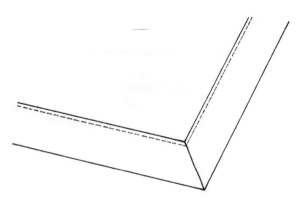

ORGANDIE BORDER NAPKIN

Cut the napkin fabric 40 cm (15¾ in) square. Cut the organdie borders 9 cm (3½ in), for a finished width of 3 cm (1¼ in), by the length of the napkin fabric plus twice the finished border. Make and stitch the borders as in Double mitred border, page 22, trimming all the seam allowances to 6 mm (¼ in) as they are stitched.

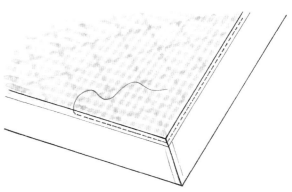

Silk table runner with tassel

This sumptuous silk table runner is lined edge to edge and is trimmed with a matching velvet ribbon. The points at each end are decorated with an elegant beaded tassel. The measurements given make a table runner with a finished size of 90 x 30 cm (35½ x 12 in).

MATERIALS

Silk fabric
Lining fabric
Pencil or marker
Ruler
Sewing thread
Velvet ribbon, 2 m (2¼ yds)
2 tassels

CUTTING OUT

1.5 cm (⅝ in) seam allowances are included unless instructions state otherwise.

Cut out a piece of fabric 93 x 33 cm (36½ x 13 in). Mark the centre of each end with a pin. Measure 23 cm (9 in) in from each end along each side edge and mark with a pin. Draw lines between the central pins and the side pins. Cut the fabric along the marked lines to make the pointed ends (diagram 1). Mark and cut both ends of the lining in the same way.

DIAGRAM 1

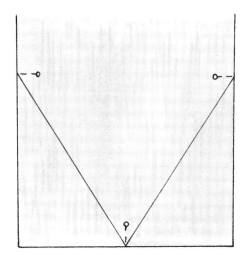

1 Place the lining and fabric right sides facing with raw edges level. Stitch together 1.5 cm (⅝ in) from the raw edges, leaving a 15 cm (6 in) opening on one long edge (diagram 2).

DIAGRAM 2

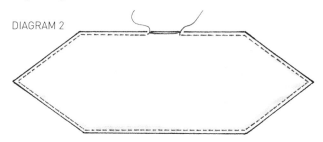

2 Trim the corners and turn the runner right side out. Press the seam allowance to the inside along the opening and slip stitch the opening edges together. Pin and tack (baste) the velvet ribbon around the outer edge. Stitch the ribbon in place along both long edges. Stitch a tassel to the point at each end (diagram 3).

DIAGRAM 3

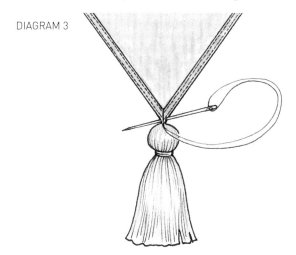

Table runner with organza border

The elegant oblong table runner has a fine linen centre panel surrounded by a wide mitred border made from gold organza. The finished runner is 41 cm (16 in) wide.

MATERIALS
Linen fabric for centre panel
Organza border fabric
Sewing thread

CUTTING OUT
1.5 cm (⅝ in) seam allowances are included unless instructions state otherwise.

Cut out two centre panels 28 cm (11 in) wide x the required length minus 13 cm (5⅛ in). For the border, cut four strips 19 cm (7½ in) wide x the required length, see Double mitred border, page 22.

1 Stitch the strips together to form a double mitred border. Trim the mitre seams to 5 mm (¼ in) and press them open. Press the border with raw edges level and right sides outside. With right sides facing, stitch both raw edges of the border together to the outer edge of the front centre panel. Press the seam toward the centre panel (diagram 1).

DIAGRAM 1

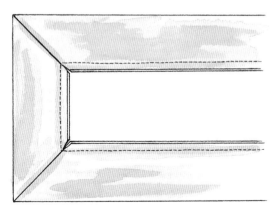

2 Press the seam allowance to the wrong side around the back centre panel. Place this panel to the wrong side of the runner and stitch in place by hand along the line of the previous stitching (diagram 2).

DIAGRAM 2

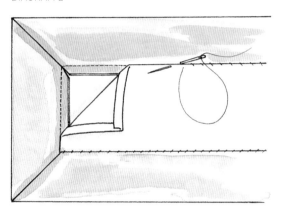

Beds

Buttoned pillowcase

The stylish buttoned pillowcases have deep hems on the two front panels that overlap and button together. The end panels are made in contrasting fabric to co-ordinate with the buttoned duvet cover on page 85.

MATERIALS

Cotton or polycotton sheeting
Sewing thread
3 buttons, 2 cm (¾ in) in diameter

CUTTING OUT

1.5 cm (⅝ in) seam allowances are included unless instructions state otherwise.

For the pillowcase back, measure the length and width of the pillow and add on 3 cm (1¼ in) to each measurement. Cut out a piece of fabric to this size. Cut the front end panel to the same width and 35 cm (13¾ in) deep. Cut the main front panel the same width as the back and 2.5 cm (1 in) longer.

1 Press and stitch a double 7.5 cm (3 in) hem to the wrong side along one long edge of the front end panel and along one short edge of the main front panel (diagram 1).

DIAGRAM 1

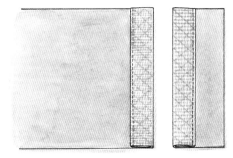

2 Mark three buttonhole positions centrally on the hem of the front end panel, placing one buttonhole at the centre of the hem and one on each side, midway between the central one and the edge. Stitch the buttonholes at right angles to the edge (diagram 2).

NOTE

A standard pillowcase measures
75 x 50 cm (29½ x 19¾ in)

DIAGRAM 2

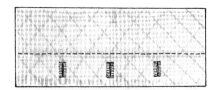

3 Place the front end panel to one end of the pillowcase back with right sides facing and raw edges level. Place the main front panel to the other end of the back in the same way, so that the hems overlap. Stitch the front panels to the back around all four edges (diagram 3).

DIAGRAM 3

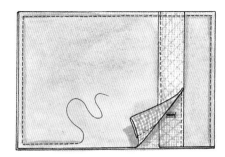

4 Trim the seam to 1 cm (⅜ in) and zigzag stitch the edges together to prevent fraying. Turn the pillowcase right side out and press the seam at the edge.

5 Stitch buttons to the main front panel hem to correspond with the buttonholes, placing the buttons to sit at the outer end of the buttonholes.

Housewife pillowcase

This simple, plain pillowcase is finished with a deep hem on the opening end and has a flap inside to hold the pillow in place.

1 Press and stitch a double 1.5 cm (⅝ in) hem across one short end. At the other short end press 1 cm (⅜ in), then 5 cm (2 in) to the wrong side to make a deep hem and stitch in place.

2 With right sides facing, fold the end with the deep hem over so that it is 16 cm (6¼ in) in from the edge with the narrow hem. Fold the projecting fabric back over the deep hem edge to form the flap (diagram 1).

DIAGRAM 1

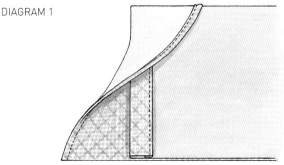

MATERIALS
Cotton or polycotton fabric
Sewing thread

CUTTING OUT
1.5 cm (⅝ in) seam allowances are included unless instructions state otherwise.

Measure the length of the pillow, double this and add on 25 cm (10 in). Measure the width and add on 3 cm (1¼ in). Cut out a piece of fabric to this size.

3 Stitch along both side edges, taking 1.5 cm (⅝ in) seam allowances. Trim the seams to 1 cm (⅜ in) and zigzag stitch the edges together to prevent fraying. Turn the pillowcase right side out and press.

Oxford pillowcase

This smart tailored pillowcase has a generously wide 7 cm (2¾ in) border around the edge of the filled area. The inner edge of the border is trimmed with a row of decorative zigzag stitching worked over an embroidery thread.

MATERIALS
Cotton or polycotton fabric
Sewing thread
Stranded embroidery cotton or coton perlé
*   embroidery thread*

CUTTING OUT
1.5 cm (⅝ in) seam allowances are included unless instructions state otherwise.

Measure the length of the pillow, double this and add on 50 cm (19¾ in). Measure the width of the pillow and add on 17 cm (6¾ in). Cut out a piece of fabric to this size.

1 Press and stitch a double 1.5 cm (⅝ in) hem to the wrong side along each short edge.

2 With right sides together, fold one short edge over so that it is 33 cm (13 in) in from the other short edge. Fold the projecting short edge back over so that it overlaps the other short edge by 16 cm (6¼ in) (diagram 1). Stitch along both side edges, allowing for seams. Trim the seams to 1 cm (⅜ in).

DIAGRAM 1

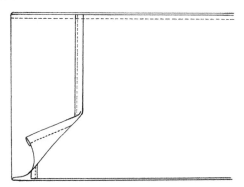

3 Turn the pillowcase right side out and press the seams at the edges. Tack (baste) the overlapping flap to hold it in place. To create the border, stitch around the pillowcase 7 cm (2¾ in) in from the outer edges. For a more decorative finish, stitch around the pillowcase again using a machine zigzag stitch worked over a length of coton perlé embroidery thread or all six strands of stranded embroidery cotton. Remove the tacking from the flap.

Basic duvet cover

This plain and simple duvet cover is easy to make and has an opening in the hem across the base edge of the cover to insert and remove the duvet. Choose a soft snuggly fabric.

NOTE

Standard duvet sizes are as follows: 135 x 200 cm (53 x 78½ in) for a single and 200 x 200 cm (78½ x 78½ in) for a double. Many furnishing fabrics are wide enough for a single duvet cover, though they may not wash well and often require a lot of ironing. Only custom-made sheeting is wide enough for a double duvet cover and has the advantage of an easy-care finish.

MATERIALS

Cotton or polycotton sheeting
Sewing thread
Press-stud tape

CUTTING OUT

1.5 cm (⅝ in) seam allowances are included unless instructions state otherwise.

Measure the length and width of the duvet, add 11 cm (4¼ in) to the length and 3 cm (1¼ in) to the width and cut out two pieces of fabric to this size.

1 Press and stitch a double 3 cm (1¼ in) hem to the wrong side along the lower edges of both pieces.

2 Place the two hemmed edges together with right sides facing. Stitch the hemmed edges together just inside the inner fold of the hem for 30 cm (12 in) from each side, leaving an opening at the centre (diagram 1).

3 Cut the press-stud tape 5 cm (2 in) longer than the opening, avoiding having a press stud near the ends. Separate the two halves of the tape.

DIAGRAM 1

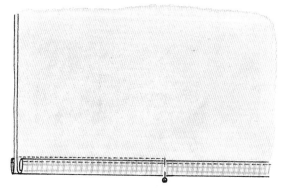

4 Position one half on one hem so that it projects beyond the opening for 2.5 cm (1 in) at each end (diagram 2). Using a zipper foot, stitch the tape in place along both its long edges.

5 Fasten the second half of the tape to the first, then pin it to the opposite hem – this ensures that the two halves match exactly. Unfasten the tape and stitch the second half in place in the same way as the first (diagram 2).

DIAGRAM 2

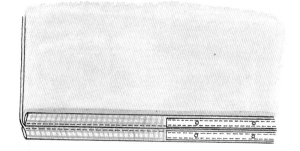

Duvet cover with border

Add a designer edge to the basic duvet cover with a crisp single mitred border stitched around a centre panel. The duvet fills the cover out to the edge of the border. Vary the look with different fabrics or combine co-ordinating checks and stripes for a country-style cover, taking care to match the pattern at the mitred corners.

MATERIALS

Cotton or polycotton sheeting
Sewing thread
Press-stud tape

CUTTING OUT

1.5 cm (⅝ in) seam allowances are included unless instructions state otherwise.

For the back of the cover, measure the length and width of the duvet, add 18 cm (7 in) to the length and 3 cm (1¼ in) to the width and cut out one piece of fabric to this size. For the front of the cover, subtract 37 cm (14½ in) from the measurements of the duvet and cut out the centre panel to this size. For the border cut strips 23 cm (9 in) wide by the required length, see Single mitred border, page 22.

1 Cut a 26 cm (10¼ in) wide strip from the lower edge of the back piece. Press and stitch a double 3 cm (1¼ in) hem across both the cut edges. Overlap the hems and make the opening in the same way as the opening on the Duvet cover with flange, steps 2–5.

2 Stitch a mitred border around the front panel, see Single mitred border, page 22. With right sides facing, stitch the duvet front to the back around the outer edges. Trim the seam allowances to 1 cm (⅜ in) and zigzag stitch the raw edges together.

Buttoned duvet cover

The smart buttoned duvet cover has a wide contrast band across its top edge that buttons onto the main front panel to form the opening. The cover is designed to co-ordinate with the buttoned pillowcase on page 76.

MATERIALS
Cotton or polycotton sheeting
Sewing thread
Buttons, 2 cm (¾ in) in diameter

CUTTING OUT
1.5 cm (⅝ in) seam allowances are included unless instructions state otherwise.

For the back of the duvet cover, measure the length and width of the duvet and add on 3 cm (1¼ in) to each measurement. Cut out a piece of fabric to this size. Cut the top front panel to the same width x 46 cm (18 in) deep. Cut the lower front panel the same width by the length of the back minus 8.5 cm (3⅜ in).

1 Press and stitch a double 7.5 cm (3 in) hem to the wrong side across the lower edge of the top front panel. Repeat across the top edge of the lower front panel.

2 Stitch a row of 2.5 cm (1 in) long vertical buttonholes centrally along the top panel hem, spacing them about 30 cm (12 in) apart.

3 Place the top panel to the top edge of the back piece with right sides facing and raw edges level. Place the lower front panel to the lower edge of the back in the same way, so that its hem overlaps the hem on the top panel.

4 Stitch together around all four edges, 1.5 cm (⅝ in) in from the raw edges. Trim the seam to 1 cm (⅜ in) and zigzag stitch the raw edges together to prevent fraying.

5 Turn the cover right side out and press the seam at the edge. Stitch the buttons onto the hem of the lower front panel to match the buttonhole positions, placing the buttons to sit at the lower edge of the buttonholes.

Throwover bedcover

This, the simplest of all bedcovers, is just a rectangle of fabric hemmed around the edges. When measuring up, remember to make an allowance for the cover to fit up and over the pillows.

MATERIALS
Heavyweight furnishing fabric, such as cotton matelassé
Sewing thread

CUTTING OUT
Measure the width of the bed and add on two drops to the floor plus 8 cm (3¼ in) for the hem. Measure the length of the bed and add on one drop to the floor plus 8 cm (3¼ in) for hems, remembering to add an allowance to fit over the pillows. If the fabric needs to be joined, add on 4 cm (1½ in) for each seam. Cut out the fabric to these measurements (diagram 1).

DIAGRAM 1

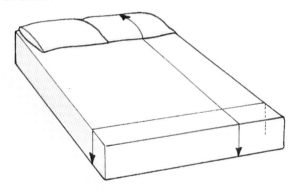

1 If the fabric is not wide enough to cut the whole required width of the bedcover as one piece, use the full width of the fabric to make a central panel and add the extra fabric required to each side. Stitch the panels together with 2 cm (¾ in) seams, tidy the raw edges together and press the seams away from the central panel (diagram 2).

DIAGRAM 2

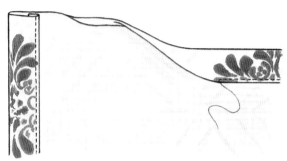

2 Press 1 cm (⅜ in), then 3 cm (1¼ in) hems to the wrong side along the side edges. Stitch the hems in place. Then press and stitch double hems along the top and bottom edges in the same way (diagram 3).

DIAGRAM 3

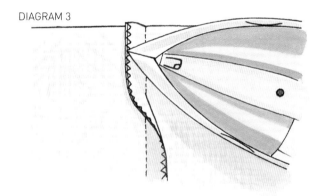

Fitted bedcover

This smart fitted cover has a straight skirt with inverted pleats. Neat piping inserted in the seam gives the edge of the main panel a crisp outline.

MATERIALS
Mediumweight furnishing fabric
Sewing thread
Piping cord

CUTTING OUT
1.5 cm (⅝ in) seam allowances are included unless instructions state otherwise.

Cut out the main panel to the required finished width plus 3 cm (1¼ in) x the required finished length, remembering to add an allowance to fit over the pillows, plus 5.5 cm (2⅛ in). Allow extra for any joins. Cut the skirt to the required finished depth plus 5.5 cm (2⅛ in). For the skirt length, double the required finished length of the main panel, plus its width, plus 20 cm (8 in) for each pleat and 8 cm (3¼ in) for hems. Plan the pleats so one is positioned at each corner. Allow extra for joins.

1 If required, join the fabric to make up the width of the main panel, using the full width of fabric for a central panel and adding narrower widths at each side. Drawing around a saucer, mark curves at the two lower corners to match the mattress shape and trim the fabric.

2 On the skirt allow 4 cm (1½ in) for the side hem, then measure the distance to the first pleat, i.e. 30 cm (12 in) for the bedcover shown here, and mark with a pin. Measure along another 10 cm (4 in) and mark with a pin, then another 10 cm (4 in) and mark with a pin. Bring the two outer pins over to meet at the central pin to form an inverted pleat, see Inverted pleats, page 26. Pin and tack (baste) the pleat in place across the top edge. Measure the required distance to the next pleat, i.e. 25 cm (10 in), then mark and form the pleat in the same way.

3 Continue joining fabric where required at the back fold of the pleats until all pleats are tacked. The distance, including hem allowance, between the last pleat and the edge of the skirt should be the same as at the beginning (34 cm/13½ in). Stitch around the top edge to hold the pleats in place (diagram 1).

DIAGRAM 1

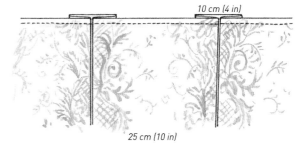

10 cm (4 in)

25 cm (10 in)

4 Cover the piping cord, see Piping, page 18. Beginning and finishing 4 cm (1½ in) in from the top edge, stitch the piping around the sides and lower edge of the main panel, clipping into the edge of the piping to fit around the curved corners.

5 Place the top edge of the skirt onto the piped edge of the main panel with right sides facing and raw edges level. Match and pin the ends of the skirt to the top corners of the panel and the corner pleats to the centre of the curved corners. Then pin the edges together between these points and tack (diagram 2). Stitch in place with the main panel uppermost.

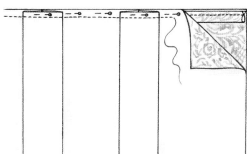

6 Press 1 cm (⅜ in), then 3 cm (1¼ in) to the wrong side to form a hem around the lower edge of the skirt and stitch in place. Press and stitch a hem across the ends of the skirt and top of the main panel in the same way. Form the pleats along the length of the skirt and press in place.

Patchwork quilt

A patchwork quilt is an eye-catching feature in a bedroom and this version, with its big, bold squares, does not take long to make. Three squares across by five down make a quilt with a finished size of 100 x 150 cm (39 x 59 in). Each square has a finished size of 25 cm (10 in) and the border is 12.5 cm (5 in) wide.

MATERIALS

Selection of cotton fabrics for patchwork
Sewing thread
110 g (4 oz) wadding (batting)
Cotton backing fabric

CUTTING OUT

1.5 cm (⅝ in) seam allowances have been included unless instructions state otherwise.

Cut out as many 28 cm (11 in) patchwork squares as required. Cut the strips for the mitred border 15.5 cm (6 in) wide x the length and width of the finished patchwork plus 25 cm (10 in). Cut the wadding and backing fabric to the size of the finished patchwork with mitred border attached.

1 Arrange the patchwork pieces as required. With right sides facing and raw edges level, pin and stitch a horizontal row of squares together along their side edges. Stitch the remaining squares into horizontal rows in the same way and press the seams open (diagram 1).

DIAGRAM 1

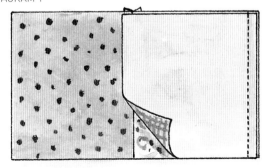

2 With right sides facing, place the top of one row to the base of the row above it, pinning the seams together before stitching so that they match exactly. Stitch all the rows together in this way and press the seams open (diagram 2).

DIAGRAM 2

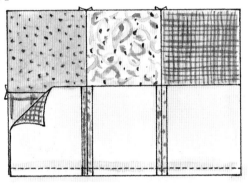

3 Pin on the borders, matching the centre of the border to the centre of the patchwork edge and working outward toward the corners. Stitch the borders in place and mitre the corners, see Single mitred border, page 22. Press the border seams open (diagram 3).

DIAGRAM 3

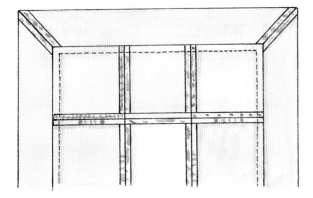

4 Place the wadding to the wrong side of the quilt and trim to fit. If the wadding needs to be joined, butt the edges together and stitch with large, loose herringbone stitch, see Herringbone stitch, page 13. Pin and tack (baste) around the edge. With right sides facing, pin and tack the backing fabric to the right side of the quilt. Stitch together around the outer edges (diagram 4), leaving a 20 cm (8 in) gap to turn through. Trim the excess wadding from the seam allowance. Trim the corners, turn the quilt right side out and arrange the seam neatly at the edge. Tuck in the seam allowances along the opening and stitch it closed by hand.

DIAGRAM 4

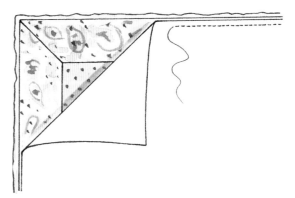

5 Arrange the three layers of the patchwork quilt evenly, smoothing the fabric flat on both sides. Pin through the layers along the outer patchwork seam, then along the lines of the patchwork squares. Tack, then machine stitch along the horizontal and vertical seams (diagram 5).

DIAGRAM 5

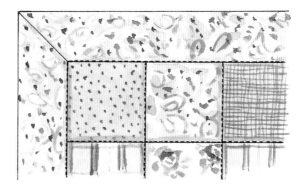

Gathered valance

A valance fits over the base of the bed underneath the mattress with a skirt that hangs to the floor to hide the bed base. Fabric with a ready-made scalloped edge gives a pretty finish to the lower edge. If you use a plain fabric for the skirt, finish the edge with a hem.

MATERIALS

Cotton or polycotton sheeting fabric
Inexpensive fabric or old sheet (optional)
Sewing thread

CUTTING OUT

1.5 cm (⅝ in) seam allowances are included unless instructions state otherwise.

For the bed panel, measure the length of the mattress and add on 3.5 cm (1⅜ in), then measure the width and add on 3 cm (1¼ in). For a bed panel with a border, see Note below, cut out the central section from inexpensive fabric and cut 10 cm (4 in) wide borders from the skirt fabric to fit around its side and base edges to make up the required size. For the skirt depth, measure from the top of the bed base to the floor and add on 6.5 cm (2¼ in) for a hemmed lower edge, or 1.5 cm (⅝ in) if using fabric with a ready-made scalloped edge. For the skirt length, add the bed width to twice its length and double that measurement.

NOTE

For economy, you can cut the central area of the bed panel, which will not be seen, from an old sheet or inexpensive fabric, adding a narrow border of the skirt fabric around the edge where it might show. If you prefer to use sheeting, you can cut the whole bed panel as one piece.

1 If required, make up the size of the bed panel by joining the borders to the edges of the central section with narrow seams, see Seams and hems, page 14. Drawing around a saucer, mark curves at the two lower corners of the bed panel and trim to shape (diagram 1).

DIAGRAM 1

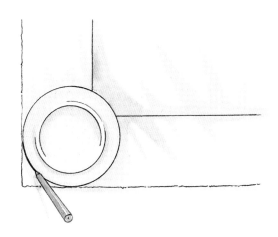

2 Cut as many fabric widths as required to make up the skirt length. Join the skirt pieces with narrow seams. If required, press a double 2.5 cm (1 in) hem to the wrong side around the lower edge of the skirt and stitch in place.

3 Measure the side and base edges of the bed panel and divide into six equal lengths. Mark with pins. Divide the top edge of the skirt into six equal lengths and mark with pins in the same way. Gather the top edge of the skirt, stopping and restarting at the pins (diagram 2). Stitch the skirt to the bed panel, matching the marked points, see Frills, page 21.

DIAGRAM 2

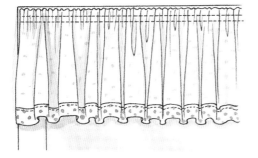

4 Press a double 1 cm (⅜ in) hem to the wrong side along the side edges of the skirt and across the top edge of the bed panel (diagram 3).

DIAGRAM 3

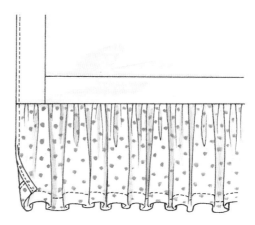

Fitted valance

The fitted valance is plain along the side and base edges with inverted pleats at the corners for a smart tailored look. This valance is made with square corners to emphasise the sharp lines.

MATERIALS

Cotton or polycotton sheeting
Sewing thread

CUTTING OUT

1.5 cm (⅝ in) seam allowances are included unless instructions state otherwise.

For the bed panel, measure the length of the mattress and add on 3.5 cm (1⅜ in), then measure the width and add on 3 cm (1¼ in). For the skirt depth, measure from the top of the bed base to the floor and add on 6.5 cm (2½ in). For the skirt length, add the bed width to twice its length and add on 84 cm (33 in).

If you wish to make the central section of the bed panel from inexpensive fabric, cut out the fabric and add borders as for the Gathered valance, page 96.

1 If required, make up the size of the bed panel by joining the borders to the edges of the central section with narrow seams, see Seams and hems, page 14.

2 Cut as many fabric widths as required to make up the skirt length. Join the skirt pieces with narrow seams. Press a double 2.5 cm (1 in) hem to the wrong side around the lower edge of the skirt and stitch in place.

3 Measure the length of the side edge of the bed panel minus 1.5 cm (⅝ in) along the top edge of the skirt. Mark with a pin. Measure along another 20 cm (8 in) and then another 20 cm (8 in) and mark with pins. Bring the outer pins over to meet at the central pin to form an inverted pleat. Tack the pleat in place along the top edge (diagram 1). Measuring from the other end of the skirt, make another pleat in the same way, see Pleats, page 26.

4 With right sides facing and raw edges level, pin the skirt around the side and base edges of the bed panel, checking that the pleats align with the lower corners. Snip the fabric at the centre of the pleats so that it fits around the corners. Tack and stitch in place.

5 Press a double 1 cm (⅜ in) hem to the wrong side along the side edges of the skirt and across the top edge of the bed panel. Stitch in place.

DIAGRAM 1

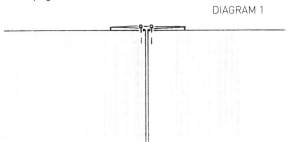

Bedhead

The pretty padded cover simply folds over the bedhead and ties at the sides. The narrow stripes have a clean country look and add charm and co-ordination to a fresh colourscheme. By replacing the lining with a contrasting fabric, you can make the bedhead reversible too.

MATERIALS

Cotton furnishing fabric
Sewing thread
100 g (4 oz) wadding (batting)
Lining fabric

CUTTING OUT

1.5 cm (⅝ in) seam allowances are included unless instructions state otherwise.

Measure the width of the bedhead and add 7 cm (2¾ in). Measure the required depth, double this and add on the thickness of the bedhead plus 3 cm (1¼ in). Cut out the main fabric, wadding and lining fabric to the established measurements. Cut out four ties 43 x 4 cm (17 x 1½ in).

1 Make the ties, see Ties, page 25. Fold the main fabric in half with right sides outside. Mark the positions for the ties at the side edges of both fabric layers, placing the top pair 15 cm (6 in) down from the fold and the lower pair 17 cm (6¾ in) up from the lower edge. Adjust the position for the ties if desired. Unfold the fabric and tack (baste) the ties to the marked positions on the right side of the fabric with their raw ends level with the raw edges of the fabric (diagram 1).

DIAGRAM 1

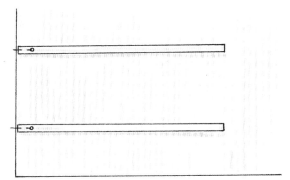

2 Place the wadding to the wrong side of the fabric and tack (baste) around the edge. With right sides facing, pin and stitch the lining to the fabric around all edges, leaving a 30 cm (12 in) opening at the centre of the back lower edge (diagram 2).

DIAGRAM 2

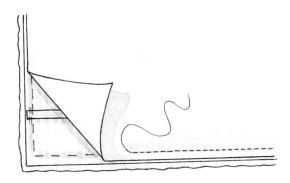

3 Trim the wadding from the seam allowances. Turn the bedhead right side out through the opening. Lightly press the seam at the edge. Press in the raw edges along the opening and slipstitch the opening closed.

Canopy

A pretty draped canopy will add bags of style to a simple day bed. The fabric is held in place by means of stitched-on casings that are slipped over wooden rods attached to the wall with brackets.

MATERIALS
Lightweight furnishing fabric
Sewing thread
3 wooden rods
3 brackets

NOTE
Choose a fairly lightweight fabric that drapes well and allow plenty of fullness. The width of the lightweight linen illustrated is about 2½ times the length of the rods; if you use a thicker fabric, you could reduce the fullness. Using the full width of fabric avoids the need for hems at the front and back edges.

1 Cut the wooden rods to the required length; the rods illustrated are 54 cm (21¼ in) long for 140 cm (55 in) wide fabric. Paint the rods white if you wish. Fix the rods to the top of the brackets and fix the brackets to the wall at the required positions. The centre rod shown here is 2 m (78 in) up from the floor and the side rods are 30 cm (12 in) lower.

2 Drape the fabric over the rods to establish the required length and mark the positions for the casings on the fabric at each rod. Cut the fabric to the required length and stitch a close zigzag stitch across each end to tidy.

3 Cut three casing strips wide enough to accommodate the rod and bracket plus 2 cm (¾ in). Press 1 cm (⅜ in) to the wrong side along the long edges of each casing. Place the casings to the wrong side of the fabric across its width at the positions marked for the rods. Stitch in place along both long edges and the front edge.

4 Press the canopy, then, starting at the back edge, thread each casing onto its appropriate rod and bracket. Arrange the fullness evenly.

Windows

Unlined tab top curtains

The top edge of these simple unlined curtains is finished with fabric tabs so that you can hang them from a curtain pole.

MATERIALS
Lightweight curtain fabric
Sewing thread

CUTTING OUT
1.5 cm (⅝ in) seam allowances are included unless the instructions state otherwise.

Decide how full you want the curtains to be. Unless a window is extremely narrow, you will need to join widths of fabric to get the required curtain width. Work out the required curtain width and add on 10 cm (4 in). Measure the required length and add on 17.5 cm (7 in). Cut the tabs twice the required width plus 3 cm (1¼ in) x 22 cm (8¾ in) long. Cut an 8 cm (3¼ in) deep facing to the required curtain width plus 3 cm (1¼ in).

NOTE
The width and length of the tabs can be adjusted to suit the fabric and the size of the pole. A heavy fabric hung from a thick pole will require larger tabs than a fine fabric hung from a thin pole. Tabs that are cut 10 cm (4 in) wide will have a finished width of 3.5 cm (1⅜ in) and are suitable for lightweight or mediumweight fabrics.

1 Join any fabric widths if required with plain seams pressed open. Press 2.5 cm (1 in) double hems to the wrong side along the side edges of the curtain and stitch in place.

2 Fold the tabs in half lengthways with right sides facing and stitch the two raw edges together. Trim the seam and press it open. Turn the tabs right side out and press the seam to one edge (diagram 1).

DIAGRAM 1

3 Fold each tab in half widthways and pin it, pointing downwards, to the right side of the curtain with its raw edges level with the top edge of the curtain. Place a tab at each side edge and arrange the others evenly in between, about 12–15 cm (4¾–6 in) apart. Pin and tack (baste) the tabs in place (diagram 2).

DIAGRAM 2

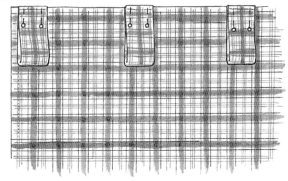

4 With right sides facing and top raw edges level, place the facing across the curtain on top of the tabs, allowing it to project for 1.5 cm (⅝ in) at each end. Stitch in place across the top edge (diagram 3).

DIAGRAM 3

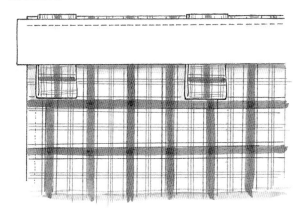

5 Press the facing over to the wrong side. If your chosen fabric is translucent, trim the fabric seam allowances to 1 cm (⅜ in). Press the seam allowances to the wrong side of the fabric along both sides and across the lower edge of the facing. Stitch the facing to the curtain along the pressed edges. Topstitch across the top edge of the facing (diagram 4).

DIAGRAM 4

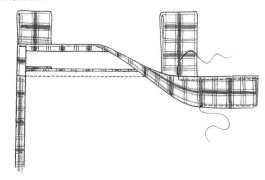

6 Press an 8 cm (3¼ in) deep double hem to the wrong side across the lower edge of the curtain and stitch in place.

Variation

This curtain, using very sheer, embroidered fabric, is particularly effective where some privacy is required without blocking out the light entirely.

Unlined curtain with fold-over top

On this pretty curtain, a section of the fabric at the top is simply folded over and attached to clip-on hooks to hang from curtain rings. Stitched tucks, which show up well against the light, are worked across the curtain on the fold-over section and above the base hem. Choose a reversible fabric, as the back of the fabric forms the front of the fold-over.

MATERIALS

Reversible sheer curtain fabric
Sewing thread
Curtain clips

CUTTING OUT

1.5 cm (⅝ in) seam allowances are included unless instructions state otherwise.

Decide how full you want the curtain to be and measure the required width. Add on 4 cm (1½ in) if side hems are required; alternatively, use the fabric selvedges as the side edges. Measure the required length and add on the depth of the fold-over plus 20 cm (8 in) for hems and 15 cm (6 in) for tucks.

1 If side hems are required, press 1 cm (⅜ in) double hems to the wrong side along the two side edges of the curtain and stitch in place.

2 At the top edge, press the depth of the fold-over section plus 14 cm (5½ in) for the tucks and turn the hem over onto the right side. At the lower edge of the fold-over, press a double 4 cm (1½ in) hem to the wrong side and stitch in place. On the right side of the fold-over, fold and press a crease 4.5 cm (1¾ in) up from the top of the hem. Stitch 1.5 cm (⅝ in) in from the crease to form a tuck, see Tucks, page 27 (diagram 1).

DIAGRAM 1

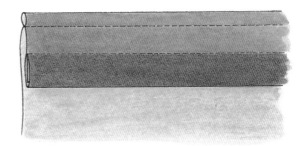

3 Press the tuck downwards. Press a second crease 4.5 cm (1¾ in) above the previous tuck stitching and stitch a second tuck 1.5 cm (⅝ in) in from the crease.

4 On the main part of the curtain, fold a double 6 cm (2¼ in) hem to the wrong side across the lower edge and stitch. Make three tucks above the hem in the same way as the previous tucks (diagram 2). Clip on curtain clips at regular intervals along the top of the curtain.

DIAGRAM 2

Unlined curtain panel

A patchwork of fine lawn panels creates a vibrant mosaic effect at this door. It has a simple fold-over casing at the top, so that it can be threaded onto a tension rod or wooden dowelling. A separate casing at the lower edge holds a length of dowelling to add weight to the curtain.

MATERIALS
Lawn fabrics
Sewing thread
Ribbons for trimming
Wooden dowelling

CUTTING OUT
Cut out as many fabric panels of varying sizes as required, allowing 1 cm (⅜ in) for seams for joining the pieces, 2 cm (¾ in) for the side hems, and 3.5 cm (1⅜ in) for the top casing. For the lower casing, cut a strip 12 cm (4¾ in) deep x the required width of the curtain panel.

2 To make a window patch, take a smaller rectangle of lawn, press the raw edges under and stitch the piece onto a lawn panel. Trim away the fabric behind the patch. Tidy the raw edges at the back with machine zigzag stitch (diagram 1).

3 Stitch double 1 cm (⅜ in) hems to the wrong side along the side edges of the curtain and lower casing. Press 1 cm (⅜ in), then 2.5 cm (1 in) to the wrong side across the top edge and stitch to make a casing. Fold the lower casing in half with the right sides outside. Stitch the casing to the lower edge with right sides facing and raw edges level, then press the casing downwards (diagram 2).

DIAGRAM 1

1 Arrange the lawn panels in vertical rows – each panel within a row should have the same width. Join the lawn panels widthways with 1 cm (⅜ in) seams to make vertical panels. If you wish, stitch ribbon trims along selected seams. Then join the panels lengthways with 1 cm (⅜ in) seams to make the whole curtain panel, adding ribbon trims if required.

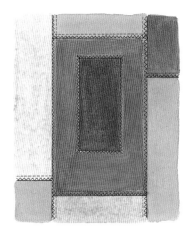

DIAGRAM 2

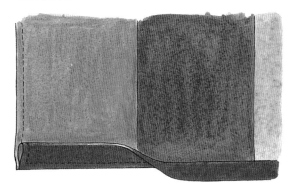

Tube-lined curtains

Tube-lined curtains are the easiest type of lined curtain to make. The lining is cut narrower than the fabric and the side edges of the lining and curtain are simply seamed together. The narrower lining pulls the fabric over to the wrong side to give the effect of a hem. However, these hems will have to be realigned and re-pressed each time the curtain is laundered.

CALCULATING FABRIC AMOUNTS FOR CURTAINS

For the curtain width, multiply the width of the curtain track or pole by the amount of fullness required by the heading tape – this is usually 2–2½ times the track or pole length. Add on allowances for side hems and joins as given for each project. Then, if necessary, round up the amount to the next full width or half width. For the length, add on allowances for the top hem and lower hem as given for each project. Multiply the length required by the number of widths to give the fabric amount. If the fabric has a pattern that needs to be matched, you will need to allow for it on each fabric width or half width.

MATERIALS

Curtain fabric
Sewing thread
Lining fabric
Heading tape

CUTTING OUT

1.5 cm (⅝ in) seam allowances are included unless instructions state otherwise.

Calculate the fabric amounts (see left). For the width, allow 4 cm (1½ in) for each side hem and 3 cm (1¼ in) for each join. For the length, add on 4 cm (1½ in) for the top hem and 15 cm (6 in) for the lower hem. If the curtains are long, you may wish to make a deeper hem. Cut the lining 4 cm (1½ in) shorter than the curtain fabric at the top edge and 10 cm (4 in) narrower than the width.

1 Join any fabric and lining widths if required with plain seams pressed open. Place the lining to the fabric with right sides facing and the top of the lining 4 cm (1½ in) below the top of the curtain fabric. Arrange the side edges level and stitch the lining to the fabric 1.5 cm (⅝ in) in from the raw edges, finishing the stitching above the hem level (diagram 1).

DIAGRAM 1

2 Turn the curtain right side out. The narrower lining will pull the side edges of the curtain over to the wrong side for 2.5 cm (1 in). Arrange the hems evenly on both side edges and press in place (diagram 2).

DIAGRAM 2

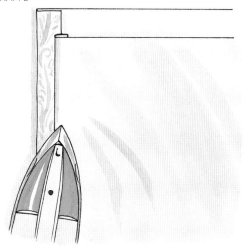

3 Press 4 cm (1½ in) over to the wrong side at the top edge of the curtain. Cut a length of heading tape 5 cm (2 in) longer than the curtain width and, with wrong sides facing, place it 3 mm (⅛ in) below the top edge of the curtain. Turn under the ends of the heading tape for 2.5 cm (1 in) at each side edge, level with the edge of the curtain (diagram 3).

DIAGRAM 3

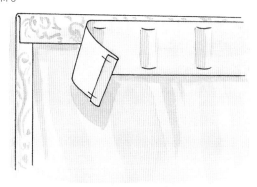

4 Stitch the heading tape in place up the side edge, across one long edge of the tape and down the opposite side edge. Stitch the other edge of the tape in the same way, so that the ends are stitched twice to ensure the cords are caught firmly in the stitching (diagram 4).

DIAGRAM 4

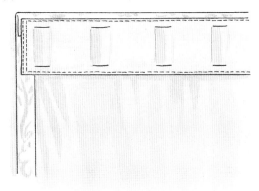

5 Trim the lower edge of the lining 2 cm (¾ in) shorter than the lower edge of the curtains. Press a 7.5 cm (3 in) double hem to the wrong side on the curtain and stitch in place (diagram 5).

DIAGRAM 5

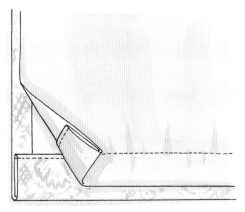

6 Make the lining hem in the same way so that it faces the curtain hem. Finish stitching the lining to the side hems by hand (diagram 6). Gather the curtains along the top edge, see Cord tidies and curtain weights, page 120.

DIAGRAM 6

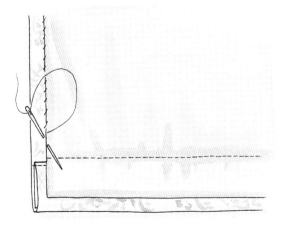

Loose-lined curtains

Loose-lined curtains are hemmed along the side edges of the fabric before the lining is attached. The lining is then stitched to the hems by hand, but left loose across the width of the curtain. You can stitch the hems at the sides and across the lower edge of the curtain by hand or machine. Stitching by hand gives a finer finish, whereas machine stitching is quicker and more durable. For large curtains, it is worthwhile mastering the machined blind hemstitch, see page 15.

MATERIALS
Curtain fabric
Sewing thread
Lining fabric
Heading tape

CUTTING OUT

1.5 cm (⅝ in) seam allowances are included unless instructions state otherwise.

Calculate the fabric amount as for the Tube-lined curtains, page 114. For the width, allow 6 cm (2¼ in) for each side hem and 3 cm (1¼ in) for each join. For the length, add on 4 cm (1½ in) for the top hem and 15–40 cm (6–16 in) for the lower hem. Cut the lining 4 cm (1½ in) shorter than the curtain fabric at the top edge and 12 cm (4¾ in) narrower than the width.

1 Join fabric and lining widths if required with plain seams pressed open. Press a 3 cm (1¼ in) wide double hem to the wrong side along the side edges of the curtain. Stitch in place by hand or machine.

2 Press 2 cm (¾ in) to the wrong side along the side edges of the lining. Place the lining to the wrong side of the curtains so that the lining edges overlap the side hems by 1 cm (⅜ in) and the top of the lining is 4 cm (1½ in) down from the top of the curtain.

3 Handstitch the lining to the side hems, finishing the stitching above the top of the lower hem. Trim the lining 3 cm (1¼ in) shorter than the fabric at the lower edge (diagram 1).

DIAGRAM 1

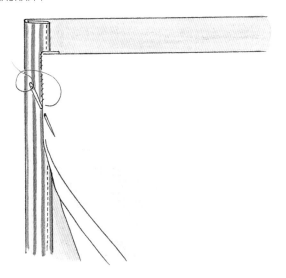

4 Press 4 cm (1½ in) to the wrong side across the top edge and stitch on the heading tape in the same way as for the Tube-lined curtains, steps 3 and 4, page 116.

5 Press a double hem of the required depth to the wrong side. Unfold the hem and the unstitched part of the side hem. At one side edge, press the corner in at an angle on a line that begins at the side edge on the top fold and intersects the inner edge of the side hem at the lower fold (diagram 2).

DIAGRAM 2

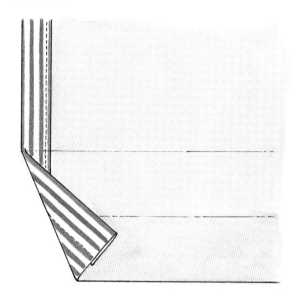

6 Refold the hem so that it forms a neat mitre at the corner. Mitre the other corner in the same way. Handstitch the mitres in place and stitch the hem in place by hand or machine (diagram 3).

DIAGRAM 3

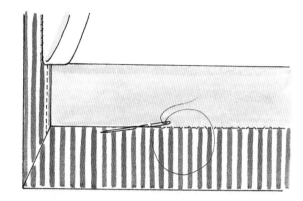

7 Make a double hem on the lining the same depth as the one on the curtain and machine stitch it in place. Finish stitching the side edges of the lining to the curtain side hems by hand (diagram 4). Gather the curtains along the top edge, see below.

DIAGRAM 4

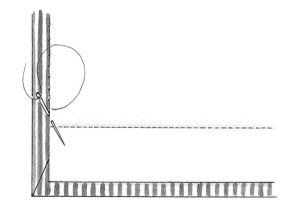

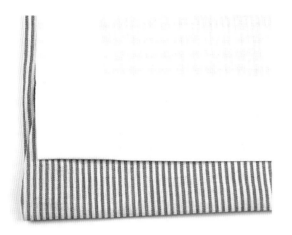

CORD TIDIES AND CURTAIN WEIGHTS

To gather curtains, pull all cords simultaneously at the centre of the heading tape and gradually push the gathers or pleats away to each side. Once the curtain is fully gathered or pleated, the cords can be wrapped neatly around a cord tidy.

Curtain weights add weight to the hems of large curtains to improve their hang. They come in two forms: round coin-like weights and long string-like weights. The coins are retained in small fabric pouches, which are stitched inside the hem at each corner and at the base of any joins. The string-like weights sit in the base of the hem and are attached with light stitching at the corners and joins.

Interlined curtain

Interlining is a layer of specially made soft fabric that is sandwiched between the curtain fabric and the lining. It adds weight to lightweight fabric and gives a sumptuous finish to the curtains. Interlined curtains also help reduce draughts and keep out the cold.

MATERIALS
Curtain fabric
Sewing thread
Interlining
Lining fabric
Heading tape

CUTTING OUT
1.5 cm (⅝ in) seam allowances are included unless instructions state otherwise.

Calculate the fabric amount as for the Tube-lined curtains, page 114. For the width, allow 6 cm (2½ in) for each side hem and 3 cm (1¼ in) for each join. For the length, add on 4 cm (1½ in) for the top hem and 12 cm (4¾ in) for the lower hem. Cut the lining fabric and interlining to the same size.

NOTE
The interlining is held in place against the curtain fabric with lines of lockstitch, see page 13, worked from the top to the base of the curtain. Curtains made from one fabric width should be lockstitched a third of the width in from each side. Wider curtains, made from more than one fabric width, should be lockstitched at each seam and twice between each seam, as well as between the outer seams and the side edges of the curtain. A thick interlining may need to be trimmed along the fold of the lower hem to reduce bulk.

1 Join fabric and lining widths if required with plain seams pressed open. If required, join interlining widths by butting the edges together and stitching across the join with herringbone stitch, see page 13.

2 Place the curtain fabric right side down on a worktop and smooth it out flat. Place the interlining on top with edges and seams lined up.

3 Fold back the interlining to the furthest seam or position of lockstitch line. Lockstitch the interlining to the fabric from 5 cm (2 in) below the top edge to the lower edge, picking up just a thread of curtain fabric so that the stitching does not show. Space the stitches wide apart and do not pull them tight (diagram 1).

DIAGRAM 1

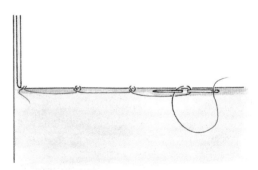

4 When the first line of lockstitch is complete, smooth the interlining back across the fabric to the position for the next lockstitch line and lockstitch in the same way. Repeat until all lines of lockstitch are complete.

DIAGRAM 2

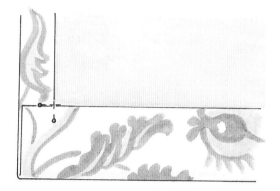

5 Fold both interlining and fabric together over to the wrong side for 6 cm (2½ in) along both side edges. At the lower edge, fold a 12 cm (4¾ in) hem to the wrong side. Mark the inner edge of each hem at the corner where they intersect (diagram 2).

6 Open out the hems and refold the corner diagonally to the wrong side between the marked points. If you are using heavy interlining, trim it along the pressed line (diagram 3).

DIAGRAM 3

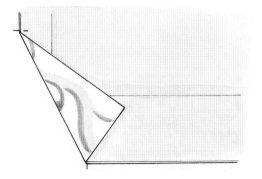

7 Refold the hems to form a mitred corner. Stitch along the side edges with long stitch, see page 13, spacing the stitches about 4 cm (1½ in) apart and taking the stitches through both layers of interlining but not the main fabric.

8 Slipstitch the edges of the corner mitres together. Stitch the lower hem with 2 cm (¾ in) long herringbone stitches (diagram 4).

DIAGRAM 4

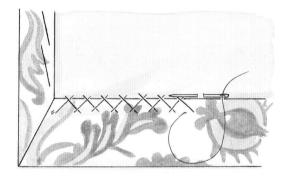

9 Place the lining centrally on top of the interlining with raw edges matching along the top edge. Lockstitch it in place in the same way as the interlining, finishing the stitching above the hem and 5 cm (2 in) down from the top edge. Trim the side edges of the lining level with the edges of the curtain. Tuck under the raw edges along the sides of the lining so that 3 cm (1¼ in) of curtain side hem shows. Pin and slip hem the lining in place along the side edges to just above the lower hem, see page 12.

10 Trim the lining to 6 cm (2½ in) longer than the curtain. Press 1.5 cm (⅝ in) to the wrong side along the lower edge of the lining. Pin in place so the raw edge of the lining is level with the raw edge of the hem and slip hem the lining to the hem along the pressed edge (diagram 5).

DIAGRAM 5

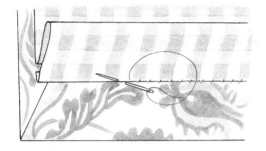

11 Allow the excess lining to fall downwards, forming a pleat. Finish stitching the lining to the side hems down to the bottom of the lining (diagram 6).

DIAGRAM 6

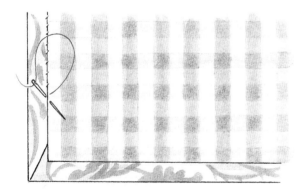

12 At the top edge of the curtain, fold back the lining and trim the interlining 4 cm (1½ in) below the top edge (diagram 7). Fold both the lining and fabric over to the wrong side for 4 cm (1½ in) along the top edge. Stitch on the heading tape in the same way as for the Tube-lined curtains, steps 3 and 4, page 116. Gather the curtains along the top edge, see Cord tidies and curtain weights, page 120.

DIAGRAM 7

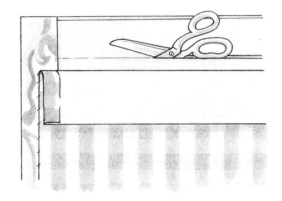

Shaped tieback

This formal style of tieback has an elegant curved shape and is made by covering stiff interfacing, pelmet interfacing or buckram with fabric that matches or contrasts with the curtain. The tiebacks can be left untrimmed or finished with cord or piping around the outer edge. They are fixed to a hook on the wall by two small rings.

TIEBACKS

First work out the required length and width of the curved tieback – the pattern illustrated is for a tieback about 28 cm (11 in) long and 12 cm (5 in) wide at the fold. Draw the pattern for half the shape of the tieback on a large piece of folded paper. Cut out the shape through both layers of paper, then open out the pattern to its full length. Try the pattern on the curtain to check the length and fit, and adjust the size and smoothness of the curve as required.

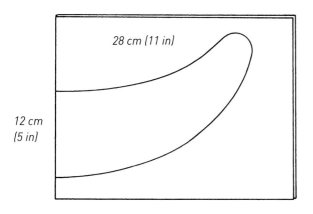

28 cm (11 in)

12 cm (5 in)

CUTTING OUT

1.5 cm (⅝ in) seam allowances are included unless instructions state otherwise.

Cut out the front fabric 1.5 cm (⅝ in) larger than the pattern all round. Cut out the lining fabric and interlining 6 mm (¼ in) larger than the pattern all round. Cut the heavyweight iron-on interfacing or buckram to the pattern size.

1 Centre the heavyweight iron-on interfacing, fusible side up, on the interlining and pin in place. Clip the projecting fabric at curves and clip out notches around the ends.

2 Fold the projecting edges of the interlining over onto the iron-on interfacing and press to fuse them in place. Take care to press on the interlining only and remove pins as you reach them (diagram 1).

DIAGRAM 1

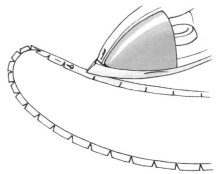

MATERIALS
Curtain fabric
Sewing thread
Heavyweight iron-on interfacing or buckram
Interlining
Lining fabric
Cord (optional)
4 small rings (two for each tieback)
2 wall hooks

3 Pin the interlined piece, fusible side up, on the wrong side of the fabric. Clip and notch the fabric edges and fuse them in place in the same way as the interlining (diagram 2).

DIAGRAM 2

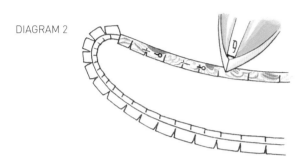

4 Clip and notch 6 mm (¼ in) into the edge of the lining. Press 6 mm (¼ in) to the wrong side all around the lining. Pin the lining to the wrong side of the tieback and handstitch in place around the edges (diagram 3).

DIAGRAM 3

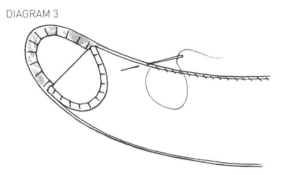

5 If you require a cord trim, handstitch the cord around the edge of the tieback, finishing the ends inside the lining in an inconspicuous place. Stitch small rings to the wrong side of the tieback at each end to fasten onto a hook on the wall.

Straight tieback

This simple straight tieback looks very effective on curtains that are partially drawn back and pulled up into a swag. It can be fastened with eyelets or rings to a hook beside the window.

MATERIALS

Curtain fabric
Sewing thread
Heavyweight iron-on interfacing
Large eyelets

CUTTING OUT

1.5 cm (⅝ in) seam allowances are included unless instructions state otherwise.

Cut the tieback 10 cm (4 in) wide by the required length plus 3 cm (⅝ in) all round. Cut the interfacing to same length but half the width.

1 Apply the iron-on interfacing lengthways to the wrong side of half the fabric. Fold the tieback in half lengthways with right sides facing. Stitch across each short edge and along the long edge, leaving a 10 cm (4 in) opening partway along the long edge (diagram 1).

DIAGRAM 1

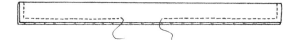

2 Trim the seams and corners and turn the tieback right side out. Press the seam at the edge and press the seam allowance inside along the opening. Slipstitch the opening closed.

3 Following the manufacturer's instructions, attach an eyelet centrally at each end of the tieback to fasten onto a hook on the wall (diagram 2).

DIAGRAM 2

Eyelet café curtain

This simple café curtain is made from a basic rectangle of fabric trimmed with a fabric flap along the top edge. It is threaded onto a narrow pole through large metal eyelets.

MATERIALS

Lightweight curtain fabric
Sewing thread
Large eyelets

CUTTING OUT

1.5 cm (⅝ in) seam allowances are included unless instructions state otherwise.

Measure the required finished size, then add on 20 cm (8 in) to the width for fullness and hems, and 9.5 cm (3¾ in) to the length. Cut out the main piece to this size. Cut the flap the same width by a third of the curtain length plus 3.5 cm (1⅜ in).

NOTE

When attaching the eyelets, work on a solid surface – concrete or paving is best.

1 Press 1 cm (⅜ in) double hems to the wrong side along the sides and lower edge of the flap and stitch in place. Place the right side of the flap to the wrong side of curtain with the top edges level and stitch together across the top edge (diagram 1). Turn the flap over to the right side and press.

2 Press 1 cm (⅜ in) double hems to the wrong side along the sides and lower edge of the flap and stitch in place. Place the right side of the flap to the wrong side of curtain with the top edges level and stitch together across the top edge (diagram 1). Turn the flap over to the right side and press.

DIAGRAM 1

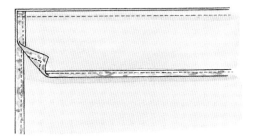

3 Mark the eyelet positions 2 cm (¾ in) down from the top and 2 cm (¾ in) in from the side edges. Space the others evenly about 13 cm (5 in) apart. Attach the eyelets through the double fabric layer, following the manufacturer's instructions (diagram 2).

DIAGRAM 2

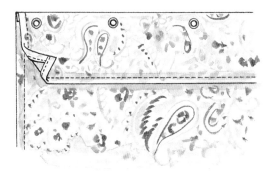

Self-frill café curtain

This curtain has a casing along the top so that it can be gathered onto a pole or wire. The narrow fold of fabric above the casing forms a pretty self frill.

1 Press a 1 cm (⅜ in) double hem to the wrong side along both side edges of the curtain and stitch in place.

2 Press 1 cm (⅜ in), then 6 cm (2¼ in) to the wrong side across the top edge. Stitch along the pressed edge and again 3 cm (1¼ in) above it to form a casing (diagram 1).

DIAGRAM 1

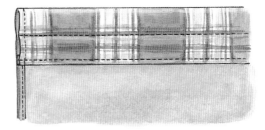

3 At the lower edge, press a double 4 cm (1½ in) hem to the wrong side and stitch in place.

MATERIALS
Lightweight curtain fabric
Sewing thread
Curtain pole or tension rod

CUTTING OUT
1.5 cm (⅝ in) seam allowances are included unless instructions state otherwise.
 Measure the width across the pole and the required length from the pole to the sill. Cut the curtain twice the pole width x the required length plus 18 cm (7 in).

Café curtain with ties

Fabric ties are used to attach this stylish curtain to a pole. The fabric is finished with a scalloped edge or an alternative hem could be made.

MATERIALS

Lightweight curtain fabric with optional scalloped edge
Sewing thread
Tension rod or curtain pole

CUTTING OUT

1.5 cm (⅝ in) seam allowances are included unless instructions state otherwise.

Measure the required finished size, then add 14 cm (5½ in) to the width for fullness and hems. Add 9.5 cm (3¾ in) to the length, or just 1.5 cm (⅝ in) if the lower edge is ready finished. Cut out the main piece to this size. Cut a facing 2 cm (¾ in) wider than the finished size x 6.5 cm (2⅝ in) deep. Cut ties 50 x 4 cm (19¾ x 1½ in).

1 Press 1 cm (⅜ in) wide double hems to the wrong side along both side edges of the main piece and stitch in place.

2 Press 1 cm (⅜ in) to the wrong side around all edges of the ties. Press the ties in half lengthways and stitch along the long edges.

3 Fold the ties in half. With the fold 6 mm (¼ in) down from the top edge and the ends pointing downwards, pin the ties to the right side of the main piece about 15 cm (6 in) apart. Tack the ties in place.

4 Place the facing across the top edge of the main piece with right sides together and raw edges level, allowing it to project 1 cm (⅜ in) at each end. Stitch in place across the top edge and trim the seam to 1 cm (⅜ in) (diagram 1) .

DIAGRAM 1

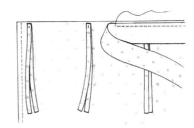

5 Press 1 cm (⅜ in) to the wrong side around the other edges of the facing. Fold the facing over to the wrong side and press the seam at the edge. Stitch around the side and lower edges of the facing. If required, press a 4 cm (1½ in) double hem to the wrong side across the lower edge of the curtain and stitch in place.

Voile swag

A length of fine linen, voile or muslin will drape beautifully over a pole to make an amazingly simple but effective window treatment. A single drape looped behind the pole at each end will frame a window perfectly. Alternatively, you can experiment with more elaborate options. First fix the pole, then drape the fabric over to establish the length required.

MATERIALS
Fine curtain fabric
Sewing thread
Sticky fixers (optional)

1 Stitch across the fabric ends with a close zigzag stitch.

2 Arrange the drape over the pole. If it slips out of place, use sticky fixers to secure the fabric to the pole at the back where they will not be visible.

Swag variations

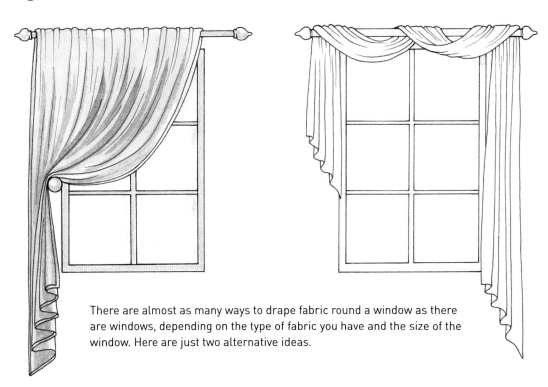

There are almost as many ways to drape fabric round a window as there are windows, depending on the type of fabric you have and the size of the window. Here are just two alternative ideas.

Pelmet with fold-over casing

This neat pelmet provides a pretty country-style treatment for a small window in a recess. It is also useful to soften the effect of a bare kitchen window, where curtains might intrude onto the work surface. The top edge is finished with a simple fold-over casing through which a tension rod is inserted to support the pelmet within the recess.

MATERIALS

Curtain fabric
Sewing thread
Lining fabric
Tension rod

CUTTING OUT

1.5 cm (⅝ in) seam allowances are included unless instructions state otherwise.

Measure the length of the rod and cut the fabric width to twice this measurement plus 3 cm (1¼ in) for side seams. Decide on the depth of the pelmet and add 7 cm (2¾ in) for hems. Cut the lining to the same width as the main fabric, but 8 cm (3¼ in) shorter.

1 Place the lining and main fabric together with right sides facing and lower edges level. Stitch together across the lower edge (diagram 1).

DIAGRAM 1

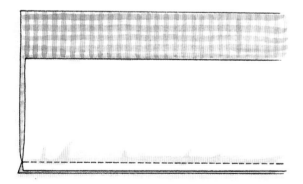

2 Open out and press the seam allowances toward the lining. Refold with right sides facing so that the seam is 5 mm (¼ in) above the fold on the lining side. Stitch together along the side edges (diagram 2).

DIAGRAM 2

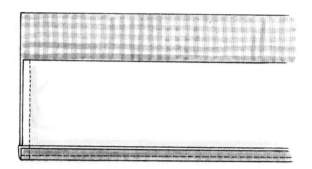

3 Turn right side out. Press 1 cm (⅜ in) to the wrong side along the top edge of the fabric. Then press 4 cm (1½ in) to the wrong side along the top edge, so that it overlaps the top edge of the lining to form a casing.

DIAGRAM 3

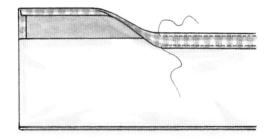

4 Stitch the casing in place along its lower edge and again just inside the top fold edge (diagram 3).

Pencil pleat pelmet

This more formal style of pelmet is finished with heading tape at the top and is drawn up into pleats or gathers. A special type of curtain track is available with an extra rail from which you can hang the pelmet. Alternatively, you can fix the pelmet with Velcro to a narrow pelmet shelf with rounded front corners. This is secured to the wall above the window.

MATERIALS

Curtain fabric
Sewing thread
Lining fabric
Heading tape
Curtain hooks or Stick-and-stitch Velcro

CUTTING OUT

1.5 cm (⅝ in) seam allowances are included unless instructions state otherwise.

Calculate the number of fabric widths required for the pelmet in the same way as for Tube-lined curtains, page 114. Decide on the depth of the pelmet and add 6.5 cm (2½ in) for hems. Cut the lining pieces to the same width as the main fabric, but 6 cm (2¼ in) shorter.

1 Place the lining and fabric together with right sides facing and lower edges level. Stitch together across the lower edge.

2 Open out and press the seam allowances towards the lining. Refold with right sides facing so that the seam is 1 cm (⅜ in) above the fold on the lining side. Stitch together along the side edges (diagram 1).

DIAGRAM 1

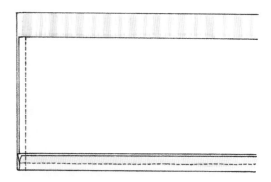

3 Turn right side out. Press 4 cm (1½ in) over to the wrong side along the top edge. Stitch on the heading tape in the same way as for Tube-lined curtains, steps 3 and 4, page 116 (diagram 2). Pull up the heading tape to the required width and arrange the fullness evenly.

DIAGRAM 2

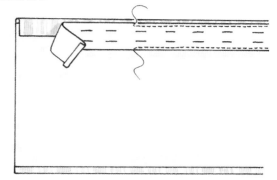

4 If you are hanging the pelmet from a track, insert curtain hooks. If you are using a pelmet shelf, cut the Velcro to fit around the edge of the shelf. Stick the adhesive side of the Velcro to the edge of the shelf. Place the "stitch" part to the wrong side of the heading tape and handstitch in place to the back folds of the pleats or gathers.

Door curtain

A lightweight door curtain is a useful accessory for a door with a glass panel, as it provides privacy while still letting the light in. A door curtain also gives a stylish look to a cupboard with a glass panel door. The curtain is held taut at top and bottom by lengths of plastic-covered tension wire secured with metal screw eyes hooked onto small screw hooks on the door.

MATERIALS
Lightweight fabric
Sewing thread
Tension wire
Screw hooks and eyes

CUTTING OUT
1.5 cm (⅝ in) seam allowances are included unless instructions state otherwise.

Measure the required width and double it for fullness. Measure the length and add on 6 cm (2¼ in) for hems. Cut out the fabric to these measurements.

1 Press 1 cm (⅜ in) wide double hems along both side edges. Stitch in place (diagram 1).

DIAGRAM 1

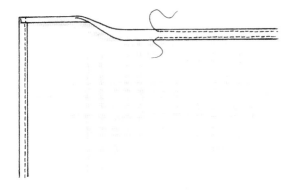

2 At the top and lower edges, press 1 cm (⅜ in), then 2 cm (¾ in) to the wrong side to make casings. Stitch in place along both edges of the casing (diagram 2). Insert lengths of tension wire into the casings.

DIAGRAM 2

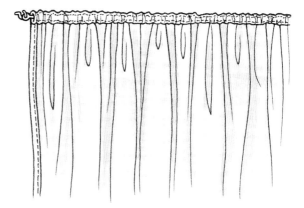

Basic roller blind

A roller blind is one of the simplest window treatments. It consists of a piece of stiffened fabric that hangs from a roller at the top and wraps neatly around it when the blind is raised. A roller blind can be hung alone or used as a sunshade in conjunction with curtains. Roller blinds are ideal for the kitchen and bathroom, where curtains might drag on a work surface or become splashed.

MATERIALS

Mediumweight fabric
Stiffening solution or spray
Roller blind kit

CUTTING OUT

Cut the fabric to about 2 in (5 cm) wider than required and 12 in (30 cm) longer to allow for the lower hem and to wrap around the roller. Ensure that the edges are straight and check that the side edges are at right angles to the top edge by using a protractor or carpenter's try square. If you do not have these tools, refer to diagram 1 – if A to B measures three units, A to C equals four units and B to C equals five units, the angle will be a right angle. Any fabric pulled or printed off grain will not roll evenly and should be avoided.

NOTE

There are two main types of roller blind: those operated by a tension roller and those with a side winder mechanism. The latter are the more widely available and usually come as a kit containing the roller, fixing brackets, winding mechanism and batten for the lower edge.

Before you make up the blind, spray or soak the fabric to stiffen it and prevent the side edges from fraying. There are various products on the market for these purposes. The soaking method is generally thought to be the more successful of the two.

The fabric should not come right to the end of the roller. Leave a gap of 2 cm (¾ in) between the fabric and the side walls on a blind to be hung in a recess.

DIAGRAM 1

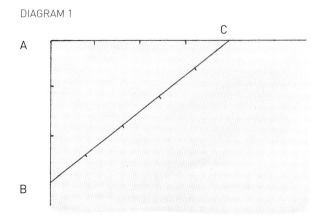

1 Stiffen the fabric with a stiffening solution or spray, following the manufacturer's instructions. When the fabric is stiffened, trim the side edges so that the blind is the required width. Press 1 cm (⅜ in), then 3.5 cm (1⅜ in) to the wrong side across the lower edge and stitch in place to make a channel for the batten.

2 Secure the fabric to the roller (which is usually supplied with a length of double-sided adhesive tape stuck to it for this purpose). Insert the batten into the channel and screw on the blind pull. Fix the blind in position inside or outside the window recess, as required.

Roller blind variations

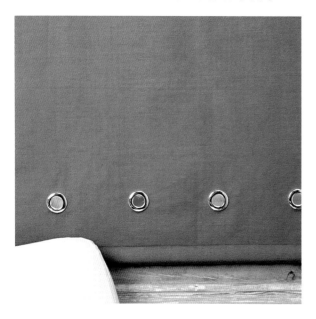

ROLLER BLIND WITH EYELET TRIM

Prepare the fabric and make up the blind as for the Basic roller blind, page 142. Determine the positions for the eyelets, placing them about 12 cm (4¾ in) up from the lower edge and spaced about 15 cm (6 in) apart. Insert the eyelets, following the manufacturer's instructions.

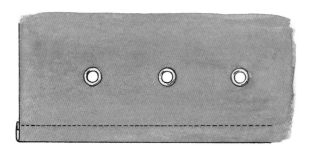

ROLLER BLIND WITH SCALLOPED BORDER

Stiffen the fabric and trim to the required width. Draw out the shape of the scallops on a paper pattern, adjusting their size to fit across the desired width. The scallops shown are 7 cm (2¾ in) deep and 38 cm (15 in) wide. Cut a 5 cm (2 in) wide bias strip and bind the scalloped edge, see Bias binding, page 16. With right sides facing, fold the blind 7 cm (2¾ in) above the top of the binding and stitch 3.5 cm (1⅜ in) in from the fold. Press the stitched pleat down to make a channel for the batten. Make up the blind as for the Basic roller blind, step 2, page 142.

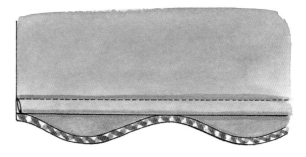

ROLLER BLIND WITH SHAPED EDGE AND DOWEL ROD

Stiffen the fabric and trim to the required width. Press 18 cm (7 in) to the wrong side across the lower edge. If the fabric is still tending to fray, apply iron-on buckram to the pressed-back turning. Stitch 5 mm (¼ in) down from the cut edge of the pressed-back turning, then again 3.5 cm (1⅜ in) below that to make a channel for the batten. Draw a paper pattern, adjusting the size and number of cutouts to fit across the width of the blind. The cutouts shown are 18 cm (7 in) wide, 6.5 cm (2½ in) deep and 5 cm (2 in) apart. Mark and cut out the cutouts. Stitch across 2 cm (¾ in) up from the folds to make channels to thread a dowel rod through. Make up the blind as for the Basic roller blind, step 2, page 142.

ROLLER BLIND WITH LACE TRIM

Stiffen the fabric and trim to the required width. Press 1 cm (⅜ in), then 4 cm (1½ in) to the wrong side across the lower edge and stitch in place. Lap the top edge of the lace under the lower edge of the hem and stitch in place. Make up the blind as for the Basic roller blind, step 2, page 142.

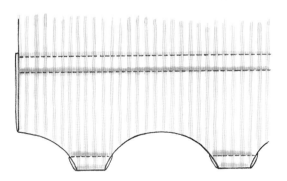

Roman blind

A Roman blind lies flat when it is lowered, but concertinas into elegant pleats across its width when raised. The pleats are created by thin lengths of dowel inserted into casings at the back of the blind and pulled up by a system of rings and cords.

MATERIALS

Closely woven furnishing fabric
Sewing thread
Wooden batten, 30 mm (1¼ in) square
Screw eyes
Stick-and-stitch Velcro
Blind rings
Lengths of dowel, 6 mm (¼ in) in diameter
Lath, 30 x 6 mm (1¼ x ¼ in)
Cleat (to hold cords in place)
Blind cord and acorn

PREPARATION

The blind is attached with Velcro to a wooden batten fixed to the wall above the window. To prepare the batten, fix a screw eye 10–15 cm (4–6 in) from each end of the wooden batten, placing it midway between the front and back edges. This will be the underside. Fix another screw eye, again placing it centrally, 1.5 cm (⅝ in) from the end where the cord will be used to pull the blind up. If the window is wide, add another screw eye at the centre of the batten. Stick the adhesive part of the Velcro across the front of the batten. Fix the batten above the window, using a level to ensure it is straight. Fix the cleat to the wall.

CUTTING OUT

1.5 cm (⅝ in) seam allowances are included unless instructions state otherwise.

Decide how many casing rods you will need: Allow 25–33 cm (10–13 in) between the rods and half this distance between the lower hem and the first casing.

For the width of the blind, measure across the front of the batten and add on 10 cm (4 in). For the length, measure from the top of the batten to the window sill, add on 3 cm (1¼ in) for each dowel casing and 7 cm (2¾ in) for turnings.

1 Press 1 cm (⅜ in), then 4 cm (1½ in) deep hems to the wrong side along both side edges. Stitch the hems in place close to the inner fold (diagram 1).

2 Press a 1 cm (⅜ in), then 5 cm (2 in) hem to the wrong side across the lower edge. Stitch the hem in place close to the inner fold. Leave the side edges of the hem open (diagram 1).

DIAGRAM 1

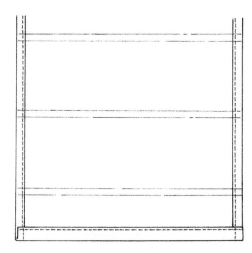

3 Mark the casing positions on the wrong side of the fabric with two parallel lines spaced 3 cm (1¼ in) apart (diagram 1).

4 With right sides together, fold the fabric along the centre between the lines so that the lines match. Stitch along the lines to form 1.5 cm (⅝ in) deep casings. Stitch all the casings in this way.

5 Using a double thread, stitch a ring to the fold of each casing 10–15 cm (4–6 in) in from each side edge on a narrow blind, to line up with the screw eye (diagram 2).

DIAGRAM 2

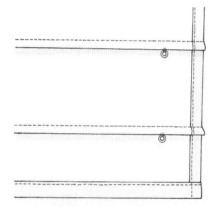

6 Press 1 cm (⅜ in) to the wrong side across the top edge of the blind. Pin the "stitch" half of the Velcro across the top edge to cover the turning and stitch in place around all four edges (diagram 3).

DIAGRAM 3

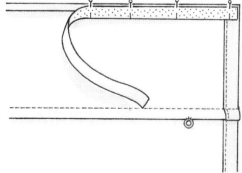

7 Insert a length of dowel into each casing and handstitch the ends of the casings closed. Insert the lath into the hem at the lower edge of the blind and handstitch the ends closed.

8 Tie a cord to the lowest ring on the opposite side to the cleat and thread up through the rings to the top. Then allow enough cord to go across the top of the blind and down the cleat side to reach the cleat (diagram 4)

9 In the same way, thread a separate cord up through the rings near the opposite edge, allowing enough cord to go across and down to the cleat. This will be shorter than the first cord (diagram 4).

10 Attach the Velcro on the blind to the Velcro on the wall batten. Thread the cords through the screw eyes as shown (diagram 4). Pull the cords to raise the blind and fasten around the cleat. Trim the cords if required, thread on the acorn and knot the ends below it.

DIAGRAM 4

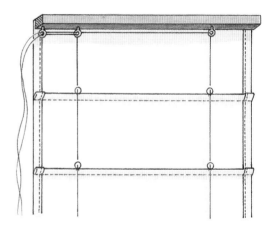

NOTE
As well as plain fabrics, vertical stripes or small prints work well for a Roman blind. Avoid horizontal stripes and any large prints as the horizontal casings will cut across the design.

Roman blind variations

BLIND WITH MITRED BORDER

A neat mitred border gives a crisp edge to a Roman blind for a smart, contemporary look. The border is most effective if it is visible when the blind is pulled up. To achieve this, allow the same distance between the finished lower edge and the first casing as between the other casings.

When cutting out, allow a seam allowance only at the side edges of the blind. Stitch the outer edge of the border to the wrong side of the blind down the side edges. Stitch the lower border to the right side across the lower edge so the stitching is level with the top of the hem allowance. Snip into the side seam allowance at the top of the hem and join the border corners, see Mitred borders, page 22. Make the hem, keeping the border out of the way, then topstitch the inner edge of the border in place. The casings are then stitched across the border.

BLIND WITH PINTUCKED LOWER EDGE

A panel of tucks adds discreet but stylish detail to a plain blind. Use bold contrasting topstitching on the right side of the tucks to highlight the detail. To ensure the tucks are visible when the blind is pulled up, allow the same distance between the finished lower edge and the first casing as between the other casings.

When working out the length of the blind, add twice the finished depth of the tucks multiplied by the number of tucks.

Make the hems at the sides and lower edge of the blind, then stitch the tucks so that the fold of each tuck is just above the stitching of the previous tuck, see Tucks, page 27.

Quick Roman blind

This quick version of the Roman blind pulls up into concertina pleats in a similar way to the traditional Roman blind, but does not use the same system of dowels and rings. Instead, just one length of dowel is used in the lowest casing and fine cords are stitched through the casings on the wrong side to pull the blind up. If you wish to make the blind firmer, you could insert stiff wires into the casings. Work out the positions and spacing of the casings in the same way as for the Roman blind, page 146.

MATERIALS
Closely woven furnishing fabric
Sewing thread
Wooden batten, 30 mm (1¼ in) square
Screw eyes
Stick-and-stitch Velcro
Dowel, 6 mm (¼ in) in diameter
Cleat (to hold cords in place)
Fine cord and acorn

CUTTING OUT
1.5 cm (⅝ in) seam allowances are included unless instructions state otherwise.

Measure the required width and add on 6 cm (2¼ in). For the length, measure from the top of the batten to the window sill and add on 2 cm (¾ in) for each casing plus 4 cm (1½ in) for turnings.

1 Press 1 cm (⅜ in), then 2 cm (¾ in) hems to the wrong side along both side edges. Stitch the hems in place close to the inner fold. Make a hem across the lower edge in the same way (diagram 1).

DIAGRAM 1

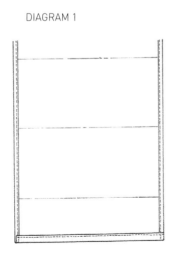

2 Measure and mark parallel lines across the blind the required distance apart for the casings (diagram 1).

3 With right sides together, fold the blind along the marked lines and stitch across 1 cm (⅜ in) away from each fold. Slip the dowel into the lowest casing and handstitch across each end of the casing (diagram 2).

DIAGRAM 2

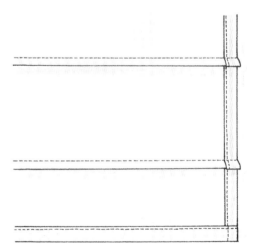

4 Press 1 cm (⅜ in) over to the wrong side across the top edge. Place the "stitch" half of the Velcro across to cover the raw edge. Pin and stitch the Velcro in place around all four edges (diagram 3).

DIAGRAM 3

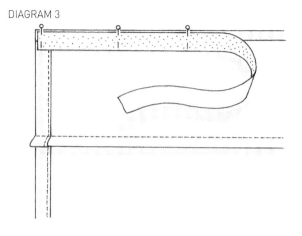

5 Allow enough cord to go up the blind, across the top of the blind and down the cleat side to reach the cleat. Make a large knot at the end of the cord and thread the cord into a needle. Stitch the cord through the centre of the lower casing, 10 cm (4 in) in from the side edge (diagram 4).

6 Then stitch through each of the casings above it in the same way. Stitch a separate cord through the casings on the opposite edge in the same way (diagram 4).

DIAGRAM 4

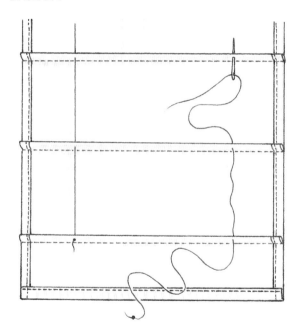

7 Hang the blind in the same way as the Roman blind, step 10, page 148.

London blind

This type of blind has a soft, ruched appearance and looks best on windows where the blind is left lowered for most of the time so that the gently gathered fabric is displayed to advantage. To retain the ruched effect even when the blind is pulled down, allow extra length when cutting out the fabric. Choose a fairly densely woven furnishing fabric for a London blind – plains and small prints work well.

MATERIALS

Closely woven furnishing fabric
Sewing thread
Wooden batten, 30 mm (1¼ in) square, and the length of the window width, plus 10 cm (4 in) to overhang
Screw eyes
Stick-and-stitch Velcro
Dowel or lath, 1 cm (⅜ in) in diameter
Blind cord, blind rings and acorn
Cleat (to hold cords in place)
2 tassels (optional)

PREPARATION

Prepare the batten for hanging in the same way as for the Roman blind, page 146, but aligning the screw eyes with the rings.

CUTTING OUT

1.5 cm (⅝ in) seam allowances are included unless instructions state otherwise.

For the width of the blind, measure across the front of the batten and add on 40 cm (16 in) for the pleats and side hems. For the length, measure from the top of the batten to the window sill and add on 6 cm (2¼ in).

1 Press 1 cm (⅜ in), then 4 cm (1½ in) hems to the wrong side around the side and lower edges of the blind. Mitre the corners as in Mitred hem, page 23. Stitch the hems in place (diagram 1).

2 On the wrong side of the top edge, measure and mark 20 cm (8 in) and 35 cm (13¾ in) in from one side edge. Measure and mark the same distances in from the other side edge (diagram 1).

DIAGRAM 1

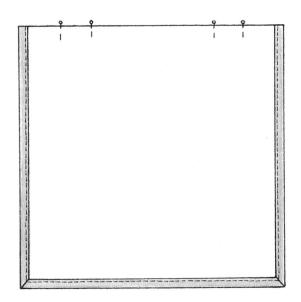

3 Fold the fabric vertically with right sides facing to match the first two marks. Stitch for 5 cm (2 in) down from the top edge to form an inverted pleat. Stitch a second inverted pleat at the other side of the fabric in the same way (diagram 2).

4 Open out each pleat and arrange centrally behind the stitching, then press in place just at the top, see Pleats, page 26 (diagram 2).

DIAGRAM 2

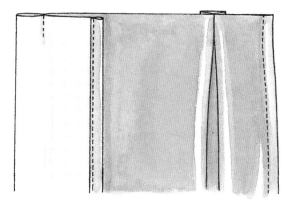

5 Press 1 cm (³⁄₈ in) to the wrong side across the top edge of the blind. Pin the "stitch" part of the Velcro across the top edge to cover the turning and stitch in place around all four edges (diagram 3).

DIAGRAM 3

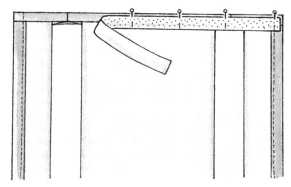

6 On the wrong side, lightly mark a line 20 cm (8 in) in from each side edge in line with the centre of the pleats. Start 10 cm (4 in) above the lower edge and stitch on rings spaced at 20 cm (8 in) intervals, ending at least 10 cm (4 in) below the base of the pleat stitching (diagram 4).

DIAGRAM 4

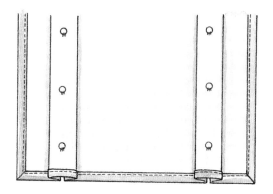

7 Cut the dowel or lath to match the length between the centre of the pleats at the top. Cut a fabric strip 7 cm (2¾ in) wide to the same length plus 3 cm (1¼ in). Fold the fabric strip in half lengthways with right sides together and raw edges level. Stitch across one short end and the long edge 1 cm (³⁄₈ in) in from raw edges to make a casing (diagram 5).

DIAGRAM 5

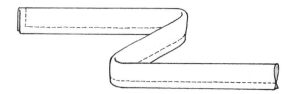

8 Turn the strip right side out and press. Insert the dowel or lath into the casing. Tuck the raw ends of the fabric to the inside and slipstitch them together neatly.

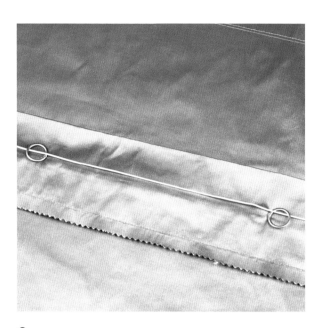

10 Stitch tassels to the lower edge of the blind hem in line with the rings at the centre of the pleats. Thread the cord and hang the blind in the same way as for the Roman blind, steps 8–10, page 148.

NOTE
If you need to join the fabric to make up the width required, place the seams at the back folds of the pleats.

9 Place the casing to the wrong side of the blind just below the lower rings and handstitch each end of the casing to the blind (diagram 6).

DIAGRAM 6

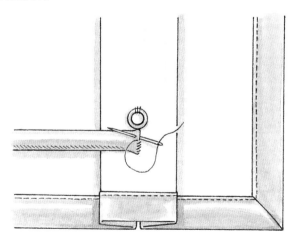

Fabric glossary

Batiste
Fine, sheer, plain woven fabric, usually cotton, used for lightweight curtains.

Broderie Anglaise
A decorative embroidered cotton fabric with punched embroidered holes available as both a fabric and edging trim. Available in white and pastel colours and used as a trim on towels, pillowcases and tablecloths.

Calico
A cheap, plain cotton fabric available in various weights and usually in an unbleached cream colour. It creases easily and may shrink when washed. Used for inner cushion and pillow covers and trial items.

Cambric
A fine, firm, closely woven plain-weave cotton fabric. Used for inner covers on cushions, pillows and duvets.

Chambray
A fine, woven, cotton fabric with white weft threads and a single colour for the warp threads (often blue). The effect is of a fine denim. Used for cushions, curtains and tablecloths.

Chenille
A soft fabric with a thick, velvety pile. Originally made from wool or cotton, it can now also be synthetic. Used for throws, bedcovers and curtains.

Chintz
Mediumweight woven cotton fabric, often printed with a bold floral design, with shiny glazed finish. Used for cushions, curtains, tablecloths and chair covers.

Corduroy
A hard-wearing pile fabric with distinctive lengthways cords of pile, available in different weights, from lightweight needlecord to heavyweight elephant cord. Used for cushions.

Crushed velvet
A velvet pile fabric, processed to flatten the pile so the tufts lay in different directions to give an interesting texture. Used for cushions, curtains and bedcovers.

Damask
A firmly woven, self-patterned fabric made on a jacquard loom usually from cotton or a combination of fibres. Traditionally used for tablecloths and napkins.

Denim
Very hardwearing twill-weave, cotton fabric traditionally with white weft threads and blue warp threads, which give a mottled, faded look. Used for cushions, curtains and chair seat covers.

Domette
A very soft, open-weave fabric with a napped surface. Made from cotton or synthetic fibres, domette is used as an interlining between the fabric and the lining in curtains, to add warmth and very light padding.

Drill
A hardwearing, twill-weave, cotton fabric usually plain dyed. Made in various weights. Used for cushions and chair covers.

Flannel
A soft, plain or twill-weave fabric with a flat napped surface usually made from wool. Used for throws, bedcovers and cushions.

Georgette
A fine fabric with a crêpe texture that drapes well and is used for sheer curtains and bed drapes.

Gingham
Lightweight, cotton fabric with white and a single-coloured thread woven to form a characteristic check pattern. Available in checks of varying size. Used for lightweight curtains and tablecloths.

Hopsack
A coarse-weave, mediumweight fabric made using two yarns in each direction. Can be made from wool, cotton or synthetic fibres. Used for throws and bedcovers.

Lawn
A lightweight, plain weave, soft cotton fabric used for sheer curtains and bed drapes.

Linen
A very strong fabric with a high lustre, made from fibres from the flax plant. Linen fabrics are available in all weights from fine lawn to heavy furnishing fabrics. Most linens crease

easily. Used for all types of soft furnishing from window drapes to chair covers.

Lining
A secondary fabric used to back curtains or other fabric items, to improve drape and cut out light, or provide a neat backing. A firmly woven cotton sateen is the most usual and it comes in a range of colours.

Matelassé
A thick double cloth with a quilted effect; it is woven from a double set of warp and weft threads thatinterlink at intervals producing the quilted effect. Used for cushions, throws and bedcovers.

Organdie
A very sheer, cotton fabric with a crisp finish that may be removed with washing. It creases very easily. Used for edgings and speciality cushion covers.

Organza
A very sheer, fine fabric similar to organdie but made from silk, viscose or polyester fibres. It creases very easily. Used for edgings and speciality cushion covers.

Piqué
A crisp, light- to mediumweight cotton fabric, often plain white, with a textured surface of fine ribs or a small geometric pattern. Used for tablecloths, napkins, cushions and curtains.

Polycotton
A fabric, usually plain weave, made from a mix of polyester and cotton fibres. This combines the comfort and absorbency of cotton with the crease-resistance and strength of polyester. Used for bedding.

Polyester
A versatile synthetic fibre, polyester can be spun to imitate the natural fibres – cotton, wool, silk and linen. It is strong and crease-resistant and is often mixed with natural fibres to add these qualities.

Poplin
A mediumweight, hardwearing, plain weave fabric with a slight surface sheen. It is usually made from cotton, or a mixture of polyester and cotton fibres. Used for sheeting, pillowcases and duvet covers.

Sateen
A strong, plain cotton fabric woven to give a shiny smooth surface on the right side and a matt finish on the wrong side. It is mainly used for lining curtains.

Sheeting
An extra wide fabric, usually a polyester/cotton mixture, produced especially wide enough to make sheets and duvet covers.

Silk
Soft but strong, silk fibres are obtained from the cocoons of silk worms. Silk fibres absorb dyes easily to produce a good range of deep colours and can be woven into various fabrics. Used for cushion covers, table runners and curtains.

Silk dupion
A mediumweight fabric with a fine but uneven slub weave caused by the natural thickening of the silk fibres in some areas. Used for cushion covers, table runners and curtains.

Toile de jouy
A traditional cotton print in a single colour on a beige or off-white background. The prints typically show romantic rustic scenes of figures and foliage. Used for curtains, cushions, tablecloths and chair covers.

Twill
A type of weave that forms diagonal lines on the right side of the fabric. There are various types of twill weaves and any fibres can be woven this way.

Velvet
A woven fabric with a surface pile. Originally made from silk, now it is often made from cotton or polyester. Used for cushions, curtains and throws.

Voile
A fine, lightweight, slightly open-weave fabric made from cotton, polyester or a mixture of the two. Used for sheer curtains and bed drapes.

Wool
Made from sheep's fleece, woollen fabrics are hard wearing, hairy and warm, and easy to mould. Wool, like silk, can be made into many different fabrics and weights varying from very fine to heavyweight. Most often used for blankets, throws, bedcovers or cushion covers.

Suppliers and useful addresses

UK

Fabrick.com
Tel: 01620 842841
www.fabrick.com
Online supplier of fabrics by British and European designers. Also supplies trimmings and interior accessories.

Fabric World
Sutton, Surrey
Tel: 020 8643 5127
www.fabricworldlondon.co.uk
Fabric stockists, also available mail order by email.

G P & J Baker
Chelsea Harbour Design Centre
Chelsea Harbour
London, SW10 0XF
Tel: 020 7351 7760
www.gpjbaker.co.uk
Suppliers of top quality curtain and soft furnishing fabrics.

John Lewis
Stores nationwide
Tel: 020 7629 7711
www.johnlewis.com
Stocks a range of furnishing fabrics and accessories. Visit the website for details of branches nationwide.

Lewis & Wood
Woodchester Mill
North Woodchester, Stroud
Gloucestershire, GL5 5NN
Tel: 01453 878517
www.lewisandwood.co.uk
Suppliers of fine furnishing fabrics and wallpapers.

MacCulloch & Wallis Limited
25–26 Dering Street
London, W1R 0BH
Tel: 020 7629 0311
www.macculloch-wallis.co.uk
Stockists of a range of fabrics, sewing equipment and haberdashery supplies.

Malabar
Studio 4, Bakery Place
119 Altenburg Gardens
London, SW11 1JQ
Tel: 020 7501 4200
www.malabar.co.uk
Designer and stockist of fabrics available through selected stockists.

Marvic Textiles Ltd
Showroom G26
Design Centre Chelsea Harbour
London, SW10 0XE
Tel: 020 8993 0191
www.marvictextiles.co.uk
Large range of fabrics available for soft furnishing and upholstery.

Online Fabrics
388–394 Foleshill Road
Coventry, CV6 5AN
Tel: 024 7668 7776
www.online-fabrics.co.uk
Large online supplier of fabric.

AUSTRALIA

Lincraft
31–33 Alfred Street (Head Office)
Blackburn, Victoria 3130
Tel: 1800 640 107
www.lincraft.com.au
Major fabric, sewing and craft retailer. Branches nationwide. Online supplier.

Spotlight
Head Office, 100 Market Street
South Melbourne, Victoria 3205
Tel: 1300 305 405
www.spotlight.com.au
Fabric and craft superstores, branches nationwide. Visit the website or phone for mail order delivery.

SOUTH AFRICA

Lifestyle Fabrics, Curtain and Linen
11/13 Picton Road
Parow 7500, Cape Town
Tel/fax: 021 930 5170
www.lifestylefabrics.co.za
Good range of fabric and soft furnishing materials.

Classic Textiles
126 Archary Rd, Clairwood
Durban, 4052
Tel: 031 465 9016
A comprehensive range of fabrics, haberdashery and curtain equipment.

NEW ZEALAND

Spotlight Stores
www.spotlight.net.nz
Large selection of fabrics and haberdashery items.

Fabric & Curtain Barn
Mt Wellington (09) 573 1919
Henderson (09) 838 6481
New Lynn (09) 826 3075
Wairau Road (09) 441 2206
Fabrics and accessories for soft furnishings and curtain making.

Index